Talk Yourself into Greatness

Kevin B DiBacco

Copyright © 2024 by Kevin B. DiBacco
All rights reserved.
No portion of this book may be reproduced in any form without written permission from the publisher or author, except as permitted by U.S. copyright law.

Staten House

Table of Contents

DISCLAIMER

No part of this publication may be reproduced in any form or by any means, including printing, scanning, photocopying, or otherwise, without the prior written permission of the copyright holder. The author has tried to present information that is as correct and concrete as possible. The author is not a medical doctor and does not write in any medical capacity. All medical decisions should be made under the guidance and care of your primary physician. The author will not be held liable for any injury or loss that is incurred to the reader through the application of the information here contained in this book. The author points out that the medical field is fast evolving with newer studies being done continuously, therefore the information in this book is only a researched collaboration of accurate information at the time of writing. With the ever-changing nature of the subjects included, the author hopes that the reader will be able to appreciate the content that has been covered in this book. While all attempts have been made to verify each piece of information provided in this publication, the author assumes no responsibility for any error, omission, or contrary interpretation of the subject present in this book. Please note that any help or advice given hereof is not a substitution for licensed medical advice. The reader accepts responsibility in the use of any information and takes advice given in this book at their own risk. If the reader is under medication supervision or has had complications with health-related risks, consult your primary care physician as soon as possible before taking any advice given in this book.

"The information and advice contained in this book are based upon the research and the personal and professional experiences of the author. They are not intended as a substitute for consulting with a healthcare professional. The publisher and author are not responsible for any adverse effects or consequences resulting from the use of any of the suggestions, preparations, or procedures discussed in this book. All matters pertaining to your physical health should be supervised by a healthcare professional."

Acknowledgments

To the people who have embarked on this journey of self-discovery and personal growth, this book is dedicated to you. Your commitment to creating positive change in your life is truly inspiring.

Writing a book like "Talk Yourself Into Greatness" would not have been possible without the support and encouragement of so many individuals. I would like to express my deepest gratitude to those who have contributed to the manifestation of this work.

First and foremost, I want to acknowledge Talk Yourself Into Greatness and the countless individuals who have shared their experiences and wisdom on this transformative practice. Your stories have served as a constant reminder that affirmations truly have the potential to change lives.

I am immensely grateful to my family and friends for their unwavering support and belief in my ability to create this book. Your love, encouragement, and understanding throughout this journey have meant the world to me.

A special "Thank You" goes to my editor and the entire publishing team, who believed in the importance of spreading positivity and empowering individuals through affirmations. Your guidance and expertise have been invaluable in shaping this book into its final form.

I would also like to extend my appreciation to the readers of my previous works, who have inspired me to continue sharing my thoughts and insights. Your feedback and engagement have fueled my passion for writing, and I am forever grateful for your ongoing support.

Lastly, I want to express my heartfelt thanks to the niche of "Talk Yourself Into Greatness". Your dedication to personal growth and self-improvement has created a vibrant community of individuals striving to live their best lives. It is an honor to be a part of this community and to contribute to your journey towards positivity and fulfillment.

To all the people who have played a role in the creation of this book, whether through direct collaboration or silent encouragement, your presence has been deeply meaningful. This book stands as a testament to the power of unity and the potential for growth that lies within each of us.

May "Talk Yourself Into Greatness" serve as a guiding light on your path towards self-discovery, personal growth, and a life filled with positivity.

About the author

Kevin's Remarkable Journey of Strength and Resilience

Kevin's lifelong passion for powerlifting and fitness has been nothing short of remarkable. Though the journey has been marked by numerous injuries and surgeries, Kevin has persevered with unwavering determination. His medical history reads like an orthopedic textbook: 6 knee operations, 2 major back surgeries, 2 hip replacements, brain surgery and brain radiation. But no amount of adversity could extinguish Kevin's inner fire and drive.

At the age of 62, Kevin undertook a monumental fitness journey to shed 60 pounds, proving that age is just a number. His passion for health and fitness remained undimmed by the passing years. Through all the ups and downs, Kevin persevered with an indomitable spirit.

He now aims to share his hard-won wisdom with others who are facing adversity. Drawing from his experiences, Kevin developed "ISOQUICK STRENGTH," a program designed to help people rebound after setbacks. He recognized that overcoming difficulties requires both physical and mental strength.

Kevin spreads his message of resilience and determination through a blog, books, and his personal mantra: "Those who quit will always fail." These simple yet powerful words encapsulate his incredible journey. After 37 remarkable years as a filmmaker, and 5 worldwide film distribution deals, Kevin now uses his gifts as a published author to share inspirational stories. With his latest release, "The Gabardine Gang," and his three best-selling books in 2024, "HYSOMETRICS," "Indie Filmmaking in the REAL WORLD," and "Hold the Power,"

Kevin continues to inspire and motivate readers around the world.

Earning the moniker "Life Warrior," Kevin stands as a shining example of the human capacity to overcome any adversity. His unwillingness to ever quit or back down, no matter the obstacles faced, is a testament to the motto he lives by: "A Life Warrior is willing to do whatever it takes to overcome life's challenges."

Kevin's journey has not been linear or easy. But through perseverance, inner strength, and an unbreakable warrior spirit, he has overcome obstacles that would have defeated lesser men. Though battered and bruised, Kevin stands tall as a shining example of human potential. His story is one of courage, resilience, and the power of embracing life's challenges with an open heart.

Kevin has used the visualization technique countless times. Many of his film projects were shot in his head long before filming began. During that time, Kevin has used visualization to produce Movies, TV shows, Documentaries, Music Videos and even as an Author. Before his career in film, he was a successful powerlifter that used 'visualization' and 'positive thinking' techniques when competing. To this day, visualization and affirmations are a tool Kevin uses regularly. Kevin has a motto that he lives by, "If you can see it, you can do it".

After a remarkable 37-year career as a filmmaker and video producer, Kevin now wields the mighty pen to craft captivating stories in the form of books.

Chapter 1: Introduction to Affirmations

What are Affirmations?

In the world of self-improvement and personal growth, affirmations have become a powerful tool for transforming lives and cultivating a positive mindset. Affirmations are positive statements or mantras that you repeat to yourself regularly, intending to manifest your desires and change your beliefs. They serve as a gentle reminder of your true potential and help you shift your focus from negativity to positivity.

Affirmations are like seeds that you plant in your mind. As you repeat them consistently, they take root and begin to grow, influencing your thoughts, emotions, and actions. By affirming positive statements, you are rewiring your subconscious mind and reprogramming it with empowering beliefs. This process allows you to align your thoughts and energy with your goals, dreams, and desires.

The beauty of affirmations lies in their simplicity and accessibility. They can be practiced by anyone, anywhere, at any time. All you need is a willingness to embrace positive change and a few moments of quiet reflection. Affirmations are a powerful tool because they harness the power of your mind and focus it on what you want to create in your life.

When you consistently practice affirmations, you start to notice a shift in your mindset and perspective. Negative self-talk and limiting beliefs are replaced with optimism, self-belief, and a sense of empowerment. Affirmations help you discover your inner strength and tap into your limitless potential.

Affirmations for Life is a niche that caters to individuals who are seeking a more positive and fulfilling existence. Whether you are struggling with self-doubt, going through a challenging time, or simply want to enhance your overall well-being, affirmations can be a powerful tool to support your journey.

Through the pages of "Daily Affirmations for a Positive Life," you will discover a collection of affirmations specifically curated to address various aspects of life, such as relationships, career, health, and personal growth. These affirmations are designed to inspire, uplift, and motivate you daily.

Remember, affirmations are not just empty words; they are a declaration of your desires and a commitment to creating a positive life. Embrace Positive Affirmations and watch as they transform your thoughts, beliefs, and ultimately, your reality.

Talk Yourself Into Greatness

In our, often stressful world, it can be challenging to maintain a positive outlook on life. However, by incorporating Positive Affirmations into your daily routine, you can transform your mindset and embrace a more fulfilling and optimistic life.

Positive affirmations are statements that reflect the reality you desire and help you overcome negative thoughts and self-doubt. They serve as powerful tools to reprogram your subconscious mind and replace limiting beliefs with empowering ones. By consistently repeating these affirmations, you can train your mind to focus on the positive aspects of life, attracting abundance, happiness, and success.

Affirmations for Life is a comprehensive guide that offers a wide range of positive affirmations to enhance various aspects of your life. Whether you seek to boost your self-confidence, elevate your relationships, or attract financial abundance, this book has affirmations tailored to your specific needs.

The beauty of positive affirmations lies in their simplicity and accessibility. You can practice them anywhere, anytime, and they require no special equipment or resources. By incorporating them into your daily routine, you can gradually rewire your brain and align your thoughts and beliefs with your desired reality.

This subchapter explores the transformative power of positive affirmations in detail. It provides insights into how affirmations work on a psychological and neurological level, backed by scientific research. You will learn how to craft effective affirmations that resonate with your subconscious mind and address any underlying negative beliefs.

Looking inside, this subchapter delves into practical techniques to incorporate affirmations into your daily life. From creating a personalized affirmation routine to using visualization techniques and gratitude practices, you will discover various tools to amplify the impact of affirmations and manifest positive change.

Remember, the power to change your life lies within you. By harnessing Positive Affirmations, you can take control of your thoughts, emotions, and actions, and create a life filled with joy, abundance, and self-fulfillment.

Affirmations for Life are your ultimate guide on this transformative journey. Start harnessing Talk Yourself Into Greatness today and unlock your true potential for a positive and fulfilling life.

Benefits of Incorporating Affirmations into Your Daily Life

In the hustle and bustle of our daily lives, it's easy to get caught up in negative thoughts and self-doubt. However, by incorporating affirmations into your daily routine, you can transform your mindset and create a positive and fulfilling life. This subchapter explores the numerous benefits of incorporating affirmations into your daily life, and how they can enhance your overall well-being.

One of the primary benefits of affirmations is the power they have to shift your mindset. By repeating positive statements about yourself and your life, you can reprogram your subconscious mind to believe in your abilities and potential. This newfound confidence will help you overcome obstacles and achieve your goals with ease.

Additionally, affirmations serve as a powerful tool for self-improvement. By regularly affirming your strengths and qualities, you can boost your self-esteem and develop a greater sense of self-worth. This increased self-belief will enable you to make better choices and take actions that align with your true desires and values.

Incorporating affirmations into your daily life can also improve your overall mental and emotional well-being. By focusing on positive statements, you can reduce stress, anxiety, and negative thought patterns. Affirmations work to rewire your brain, encouraging a more optimistic outlook and promoting a sense of calm and inner peace.

Furthermore, affirmations can have a profound impact on your relationships. By affirming qualities such as love, compassion, and forgiveness, you can cultivate healthier and more fulfilling connections with others. Affirmations can also help you set boundaries, communicate effectively, and attract positive and supportive people into your life.

Another benefit of incorporating affirmations into your daily routine is the increased motivation and productivity they provide. By affirming your goals and intentions, you create a clear vision for your future and instill a sense of purpose into your actions. This heightened motivation will help you stay focused and determined, even when faced with challenges.

In reality, incorporating affirmations into your daily life can have a transformative effect on your overall well-being. By shifting your mindset, boosting self-esteem, reducing stress, improving relationships, and enhancing motivation, affirmations empower you to live a more positive and fulfilling life. Start incorporating affirmations into your daily routine today, and witness the incredible benefits they can bring to your life.

Chapter 2: Getting Started with Affirmations

Setting Your Intentions

Setting intentions is a powerful practice that can transform your life and help you achieve your goals. It involves consciously focusing your thoughts and energy on what you want to manifest in your life. By setting clear intentions, you create a roadmap for success and invite positive outcomes into your daily experiences.

Intention setting begins with self-reflection. Take some time to get in touch with your inner desires and aspirations. What do you truly want to achieve in your life? What areas do you wish to improve? By identifying your values and goals, you will be able to set intentions that align with your authentic self.

Once you clearly understand what you want, it's time to turn those desires into intentions. Write them down in a journal or create a vision board that represents your goals. Use positive language and be specific about what you want to attract into your life. Remember, the universe responds to clarity and positivity.

Affirmations play a crucial role in setting intentions. These positive statements can reprogram your subconscious mind and reinforce your intentions. Repeat affirmations that resonate with your goals daily, either silently or out loud. By doing so, you train your mind to focus on what you want, rather than what you don't want. Affirmations for life can help you cultivate a positive mindset and attract abundance in all areas of your life.

To enhance the power of your intentions, visualize yourself already living your desired reality. Close your eyes and imagine every detail of your dream life—the sights, sounds, and emotions. Feel the joy, fulfillment, and gratitude as if it has already manifested. Visualization strengthens the connection between your conscious and subconscious mind, making your intentions even more potent.

Setting intentions also involves taking inspired action. While it's important to trust the universe and allow things to unfold naturally, it's equally crucial to take steps towards your goals. Break down your intentions into manageable action steps and commit to taking consistent, purposeful action. The more aligned your actions are with your intentions, the more likely you are to manifest your desires.

Remember, setting intentions is an ongoing practice. Revlsit and revise your intentions as your desires evolve and change. Stay open to new possibilities and trust that the universe is always conspiring in your favor. By setting clear intentions and aligning your thoughts, feelings, and actions, you can create a positive and fulfilling life.

Affirmations for life are a powerful tool in this process, helping you stay focused and maintain a positive mindset. By incorporating intention setting into your daily routine, you can create the life you've always desired, one intention at a time.

Choosing the Right Affirmations for You

Affirmations have the power to transform your life and bring about positive change. They are simple yet effective statements that can help you manifest your desires, boost your self-confidence, and create a more fulfilling life. However, not all affirmations are created equal. To truly benefit from Positive Affirmations, it is crucial to choose the right ones that resonate with you and align with your goals.

When selecting affirmations, it is important to consider your specific needs and desires. Start by identifying the areas of your life that you want to improve or transform. Is it your career, relationships, health, or personal development? Once you have a clear idea of what you would like to focus on, you can begin to explore affirmations that are relevant to your chosen niche.

Affirmations for life can cover a wide range of topics, from self-love and abundance to gratitude and happiness. It is essential to select affirmations that feel authentic to you. If you struggle with self-confidence, for example, affirmations such as "I am worthy of love and success" or "I believe in my abilities" would be more appropriate. On the other hand, if you are seeking financial abundance, affirmations like "I attract wealth and prosperity effortlessly" or "Money flows to me easily and abundantly" may be more suitable.

To ensure the effectiveness of your affirmations, it is crucial to use positive and empowering language. Instead of focusing on what you lack or want to change, frame your affirmations in a way that emphasizes what you already possess or desire to manifest. For instance, rather than saying "I am not stressed," rephrase it as "I am calm and at peace."

Another important aspect of choosing affirmations is to make them believable and achievable. While it is essential to dream big, affirmations that feel unrealistic or unattainable may not have the desired impact. Start with affirmations that you genuinely believe in, and gradually expand your comfort zone as you witness positive changes in your life.

Lastly, consistency is key. Make it a daily practice to recite your chosen affirmations, preferably in the morning or before bed. Repetition is essential to rewire your subconscious mind and reinforce positive beliefs. Consider writing them down, creating visual reminders, or even recording them as voice memos to make the practice more engaging and effective.

Remember, the right affirmations have the power to transform your life. By selecting affirmations that resonate with you and align with your goals, you can harness their incredible potential to manifest positive change and create a life filled with joy, abundance, and fulfillment.

Writing Your Affirmations

Affirmations are powerful tools that can help us shape our thoughts and beliefs, ultimately leading to a positive and fulfilling life. By consciously deciding and repeating positive statements, we can reprogram our minds to focus on what we want to manifest. Writing your affirmations is a creative process that allows you to tailor your statements to your unique needs and desires. In this subchapter, we will explore some effective techniques to guide you in writing your affirmations for a positive life.

Firstly, it is important to identify the areas of your life that you would like to improve or manifest. Are you seeking abundance, love, health, or success? Once you fully understand your desires, you can begin crafting affirmations that are specific and aligned with your goals. For example, if you desire financial abundance, you can write affirmations such as, "I am attracting limitless wealth and prosperity into my life."

While writing your affirmations, it is crucial to use positive language. Instead of focusing on what you lack or want to change, frame your affirmations in a way that affirms the positive outcome you desire. For instance, rather than saying, "I am not afraid of failure," rephrase it as, "I am confident and successful in all my endeavors." By using positive language, you are signaling to the universe that you are already in alignment with your desires.

Another helpful technique is to make your affirmations personal and present tense. By using "I" or "my" and writing in the present moment, you are reinforcing the belief that what you desire is already happening. For example, instead of saying, "I will be healthy," say, "I am vibrant and healthy in body, mind, and spirit." This encourages a sense of ownership and empowers you to take action towards your desired outcome.

Keep in mind that affirmations should resonate with you on a deep emotional level. They should evoke feelings of joy, gratitude, and excitement. If an affirmation feels forced or doesn't resonate with you, it may be helpful to rephrase it or find a different affirmation that aligns better with your authentic self.

Repetition is key. Consistently repeat your affirmations daily, preferably in the morning and evening. This will help to reinforce the positive beliefs and thoughts you are cultivating. Consider using visualization techniques while repeating your affirmations to further enhance their effectiveness.

Simply, writing your affirmations is a personal and creative process that allows you to shape your thoughts and beliefs. By identifying your desires, using positive language, making them personal, and repeating them with intention, you can harness Talk Yourself Into Greatness to manifest a positive life. Embrace this practice wholeheartedly and watch as your affirmations become your reality.

How to Use Affirmations Effectively

Introduction:

Welcome to the subchapter on how to use affirmations effectively. In this section, we will explore Talk Yourself Into Greatness and provide you with practical tips on how to make the most out of these positive statements to transform your life. Whether you are new to affirmations or have been practicing them for some time, this guide will help you harness their full potential.

Understanding Positive Affirmations:

Affirmations are powerful tools that can reprogram your subconscious mind and shape your reality. By using positive statements and repeating them regularly, you can replace negative beliefs and self-doubt with empowering thoughts. Affirmations can boost your self-confidence, improve your focus, and attract abundance into your life.

1. Set Clear and Specific Goals:

To use affirmations effectively, start by setting clear and specific goals. Identify the areas of your life that you want to improve or transform. Whether it's your career, relationships, health, or personal development, be specific about what you intend to achieve.

2. Create Personalized Affirmations:

Craft affirmations that resonate with you personally. Use words and phrases that reflect your aspirations and align with your values. Make sure your affirmations are positive, present tense, and emotionally charged. For example, instead of saying, "I will be successful," say, "I am attracting success and abundance into my life."

3. Repeat Affirmations Consistently:

Consistency is key when it comes to affirmations. Repeat your affirmations daily, preferably in the morning and before bed. Consistency helps to reinforce positive beliefs and rewire your subconscious mind. Use tools like sticky notes, affirmation cards, or digital reminders to keep your affirmations easily accessible throughout the day.

4. Engage Your Senses:

To deepen the effectiveness of your affirmations, engage your senses. Visualize yourself already living your desired reality. Feel the emotions associated with achieving your goals. You can also create vision boards or use guided meditation to enhance the sensory experience.

5. Believe in Your Affirmations:

Belief is a fundamental part of using affirmations effectively. Trust that your affirmations are creating positive changes in your life. Cultivate a strong belief in yourself and your ability to manifest your desires. As you reinforce positive thoughts, you will naturally align your actions with your affirmations.

Using affirmations effectively can be a life-changing practice. By setting clear goals, creating personalized affirmations, repeating them consistently, engaging your senses, and cultivating belief, you can harness the transformative power of affirmations to create a positive and fulfilling life. Remember, the key is to trust the process, stay committed, and watch as your affirmations manifest into reality.

Chapter 3: Affirmations for Self-Love and Self-Acceptance

Embracing Your Uniqueness

In a world that often tries to fit us into molds and conform to societal norms, it is crucial to recognize and embrace our uniqueness. Each one of us is born with our set of talents, skills, and qualities that make us special and irreplaceable. The journey to self-acceptance and embracing our individuality is a powerful and transformative one.

Affirmations for Life has always believed in the power of self-love and acceptance. In this subchapter, we invite you, dear reader, to embark on a journey of embracing your uniqueness and celebrating your individuality. It is time to break free from the chains of comparison and self-doubt and step into the light of self-empowerment.

The first step towards embracing your uniqueness is to understand that no two individuals are the same. We are all beautifully different in our ways. Embrace your quirks, your passions, and the things that make you stand out from the crowd. Remember, it is in embracing our differences that we find true fulfillment and happiness.

One of the most effective tools in this journey is the practice of daily affirmations. These positive statements serve as a reminder of your worth and unique qualities. Speak them aloud every morning and let them sink deep into your subconscious mind. Affirmations such as "I am proud of who I am," "I embrace my individuality," and "I celebrate my uniqueness" will help you develop a strong sense of self-acceptance and love.

Embracing your uniqueness also involves surrounding yourself with people who appreciate and support you for who you are. Seek those who uplift and empower you, and distance yourself from those who undermine your confidence. Remember, you deserve to be surrounded by individuals who celebrate your individuality and encourage you to shine.

Furthermore, take the time to explore your passions and interests fully. Engage in activities that make your heart sing and bring you joy. Whether it's painting, dancing, writing, or any other form of self-expression, embrace it wholeheartedly. Allow your uniqueness to shine through your creativity and make a positive impact on the world around you.

Embracing your uniqueness is an ongoing practice. It requires patience, self-compassion, and a commitment to self-growth. Remember that you are one-of-a-kind, and your unique qualities have the power to inspire and uplift others. So, let go of self-doubt, embrace your individuality, and live a life that celebrates your uniqueness every day.

Celebrating Your Achievements

In our journey through life, it is important to acknowledge and celebrate our achievements. Each step forward, each milestone reached, deserves recognition and appreciation. By celebrating our accomplishments, we cultivate a positive mindset and reinforce our belief in our abilities. In this subchapter, we will explore the significance of celebrating achievements and provide affirmations to help you embrace this practice in your daily life.

The Power of Celebrating:

Celebrating your achievements is not just about throwing a party or receiving praise from others. It is a way to honor your hard work, dedication, and progress. By taking the time to reflect on your accomplishments, you reinforce positive behaviors and build self-confidence. Celebrating also allows you to appreciate the journey rather than solely focusing on the destination. It helps you find joy in the process and maintain a positive outlook on life.

Affirmations for Celebrating Your Achievements:

1. I am proud of my accomplishments, big and small.

2. I celebrate each step forward, knowing that progress is a journey.

3. I honor my dedication and hard work by acknowledging my achievements.

4. I choose to focus on my successes and let go of self-doubt and negativity.

5. Celebrating my achievements empowers me to reach for even greater heights.

6. I find joy in the process and celebrate every milestone I reach.

7. I am deserving of recognition and celebration for my efforts.

8. I celebrate not only my achievements, but also the growth and lessons that come with them.

9. I embrace my successes and use them as motivation to continue striving for greatness.

10. By celebrating my achievements, I inspire others to believe in their potential.

Incorporating Celebration into Your Daily Life:

To make celebrating your achievements a habit, it is important to integrate it into your daily life. Set aside time each day to reflect on your progress and honor your accomplishments. This can be as simple as journaling, creating a gratitude list, or sharing your achievements with loved ones. Surround yourself with positivity and celebrate the achievements of others as well. By making celebration a part of your routine, you will cultivate a mindset of gratitude and abundance.

Conclusion:

Celebrating your achievements is an essential practice for a positive and fulfilling life. By acknowledging your progress, you reinforce positive beliefs, boost self-confidence, and find joy in the journey. Use the provided affirmations and incorporate celebration into your daily routine to cultivate a mindset of gratitude and abundance. Embrace the power of celebrating your achievements and watch as it transforms your life for the better.

Letting Go of Self-Doubt

In our journey through life, we often find ourselves battling with self-doubt. This nagging feeling that we are not good enough, smart enough, or capable enough can hold us back from reaching our full potential. However, it is important to remember that self-doubt is not based on reality but rather on our insecurities and fears. It is a barrier that prevents us from living a positive and fulfilling life.

In the subchapter titled "Letting Go of Self-Doubt" from the book "Daily Affirmations for a Positive Life," we explore powerful affirmations and techniques to overcome this paralyzing emotion. Addressed to people from all walks of life, particularly those seeking affirmations for life, this subchapter aims to provide guidance and support on their journey towards self-acceptance and personal growth.

The first step in releasing self-doubt is acknowledging its presence. By recognizing that self-doubt is a product of our thoughts and not an accurate reflection of our abilities, we can start to challenge and overcome it. The book offers practical exercises and affirmations that help individuals separate their self-worth from their doubts, allowing them to embrace their true potential.

Moreover, "Letting Go of Self-Doubt" provides insights into the damaging effects of comparing oneself to others. It encourages readers to focus on their own unique journey and strengths, rather than measuring their worth against others. Through affirmations that emphasize self-compassion and self-acceptance, the book helps individuals develop a positive mindset that nurtures self-love and confidence.

This subchapter delves into the concept of fear as a driving force behind self-doubt. It provides strategies to confront and overcome these fears, empowering readers to step out of their comfort zones and pursue their dreams. By replacing negative thoughts with positive affirmations, individuals can rewire their mindset and cultivate a belief in their abilities.

"Letting Go of Self-Doubt" is a transformative subchapter that equips readers with the tools necessary to break free from the chains of self-doubt. It encourages them to embrace their uniqueness, trust their intuition, and live a life driven by courage and self-assurance. By practicing daily affirmations and implementing the techniques outlined in this subchapter, individuals can embark on a journey of self-discovery, personal growth, and a positive life.

Cultivating Self-Compassion

It is easy to become our own harshest critics. We often hold ourselves to impossibly high standards and beat ourselves up over perceived failures and shortcomings. However, it is crucial to remember that self-compassion is an essential ingredient for living a positive and fulfilling life. It enables us to embrace our imperfections, practice self-care, and develop resilience in the face of challenges.

Self-compassion is the practice of treating ourselves with kindness, understanding, and acceptance, just as we would treat a dear friend or loved one. It involves acknowledging our pain and suffering without judgment, and actively nurturing ourselves with love and care. By cultivating self-compassion, we can transform our inner dialogue and create a nurturing environment within ourselves.

One powerful tool for cultivating self-compassion is the use of daily affirmations. Affirmations are positive statements that can help reframe our thinking and foster self-compassion. By repeating affirmations regularly, we can rewire our minds to embrace self-love and acceptance.

Here are a few affirmations to cultivate self-compassion:

1. "I am worthy of love and kindness, just as I am."

2. "I choose to release self-judgment and embrace my imperfections."

3. "I forgive myself for past mistakes and allow space for growth and transformation."

4. "I honor my needs and prioritize self-care in my daily life."

5. "I am resilient and capable of overcoming any challenge that comes my way."

By incorporating these affirmations into your daily routine, you can gradually shift your mindset towards self-compassion. Begin each day by reciting these affirmations, either silently or out loud, and remind yourself that you deserve love, understanding, and forgiveness.

In addition to affirmations, it is essential to practice self-care regularly. This can include activities such as engaging in hobbies, spending time in nature, nurturing relationships with loved ones, or engaging in mindfulness practices like meditation and journaling. Taking care of your physical, emotional, and mental well-being is an act of self-compassion that will enhance your overall quality of life.

Remember, cultivating self-compassion is a lifelong journey. Be patient with yourself as you develop this practice, and remember that it is okay to ask for help and support along the way. By embracing self-compassion, you are opening the door to a more positive and fulfilling life, where love and acceptance are at the forefront of your relationship with yourself.

Chapter 4: Affirmations for Confidence and Success

Building Confidence from Within

Confidence is not something that can be bought or borrowed; it is a quality that needs to be nurtured from within. In our journey of self-improvement and personal growth, building confidence becomes an essential element. This subchapter aims to guide people in the niche of "Affirmations for Life" towards developing unwavering self-assurance and a positive outlook.

Confidence is not an overnight achievement; it is a gradual process that demands consistent effort and belief in oneself. The first step towards building confidence is to cultivate a positive mindset. Our thoughts have the power to shape our reality, and by affirming positive beliefs about ourselves, we can transform our self-perception. Affirmations such as "I am worthy of success" or "I can overcome any challenge" can help rewire our subconscious mind, replacing self-doubt with self-assurance.

Another essential aspect of building confidence is recognizing and embracing our strengths and accomplishments. Often, we tend to focus on our weaknesses and failures, undermining our abilities. By shifting our attention to our achievements and unique talents, we can boost our self-esteem. Regularly acknowledging our accomplishments, even the smallest ones, helps us realize our potential and strengthens our belief in ourselves.

Building confidence also involves stepping out of our comfort zones and facing our fears. Taking small steps towards our goals, even if they seem daunting at first, gradually builds our confidence. Each small victory adds to our belief in our abilities and strengthens our resolve to overcome challenges.

Surrounding ourselves with positive and supportive individuals is crucial in our journey of self-confidence. Being in the company of people who believe in us, encourage us, and provide constructive feedback can make a significant difference in our self-perception. Collaboration with like-minded individuals can also inspire us to aim higher and push our boundaries.

Self-care plays an integral role in building confidence. Taking care of our physical and mental well-being through activities like exercise, meditation, and self-reflection helps us develop a strong foundation of self-assurance. When we prioritize our needs and invest in self-improvement, we send a message to ourselves that we are deserving of love, respect, and success.

Additionally, building confidence from within is a vital aspect of our personal growth journey. By cultivating a positive mindset, acknowledging our achievements, stepping out of our comfort zones, surrounding ourselves with uplifting individuals, and prioritizing self-care, we can develop unwavering self-assurance and embrace a positive life. Remember, confidence is not something we find outside; it's a treasure we discover within ourselves.

Embracing Challenges as Opportunities for Growth

In life, challenges are inevitable. They come in various forms and can often leave us feeling overwhelmed and defeated. However, it is important to remember that every challenge we encounter presents an opportunity for growth and personal development. By shifting our mindset and embracing these challenges, we can unlock our true potential and live a more positive and fulfilling life.!

One of the most powerful tools we have at our disposal is the practice of daily affirmations. By incorporating affirmations for life into our daily routine, we can rewire our thinking patterns and develop a resilient mindset that allows us to face challenges head-on.

When faced with a challenge, it is natural to feel fear and uncertainty. However, by affirming positive thoughts and beliefs, we can overcome these negative emotions and see the situation as an opportunity for growth. Affirmations such as "I am capable of conquering any challenge that comes my way" or "Challenges are my stepping stones to success" can help us reframe our perspective and approach challenges with confidence and determination.

Embracing challenges as opportunities for growth allows us to step outside our comfort zones and expand our boundaries. It is through facing difficulties that we learn new skills, gain valuable experiences, and discover our true potential. Each challenge we overcome builds our resilience and strengthens our character, enabling us to tackle even greater obstacles in the future.

Additionally, challenges provide us with the chance to learn from our mistakes and make necessary adjustments to improve ourselves. By embracing these opportunities for growth, we can develop a growth mindset and become more adaptable to change. Rather than viewing challenges as roadblocks, we can see them as stepping stones towards personal and professional success.

Once again, embracing challenges as opportunities for growth is a mindset shift that has the power to transform our lives. By incorporating daily affirmations for life into our routine, we can rewire our thinking patterns and approach challenges with a positive and resilient mindset. Remember that challenges are not meant to break us, but to help us grow and become the best version of ourselves. Embrace the challenges that come your way, for they hold the keys to your personal and professional success.

Overcoming Fear of Failure

Fear of failure is something that holds many people back from reaching their full potential and living a positive life. It is a common human trait to fear failure, as we are wired to avoid any kind of discomfort or disappointment. However, allowing this fear to control our actions can hinder our progress and prevent us from achieving our goals. This subchapter aims to help you overcome your fear of failure through Positive Affirmations.

Affirmations are positive statements that can reprogram your mind and shift your mindset towards success. By repeating affirmations daily, you can break free from the fear of failure and develop a more resilient and positive attitude towards life.

One powerful affirmation to repeat is, "I am not defined by my failures, but by how I rise above them." Remind yourself that failure is a natural part of life, and it does not define your worth or abilities. Instead, focus on how you can learn and grow from your failures, using them as stepping stones towards success.

Another affirmation to embrace is, "I am capable of achieving anything I set my mind to." Believe in your abilities and trust in your potential. Fear of failure often stems from self-doubt, but by affirming your capabilities, you can build self-confidence and overcome any obstacles that come your way.

"I embrace failure as an opportunity for growth" is yet another powerful affirmation. By reframing failure as a chance to learn and improve, you can remove the fear associated with it. Embrace failures as valuable lessons and stepping stones towards success, rather than as evidence of your shortcomings.

In addition to affirmations, it is important to surround yourself with a supportive community. Connect with like-minded individuals who share similar goals and struggles. Share your fears and experiences, and learn from one another's journeys. Having a support system can provide the encouragement and motivation needed to overcome the fear of failure.

Remember, the fear of failure is just an illusion. By incorporating positive affirmations and building a strong support system, you can break free from this fear and embrace a positive life filled with growth, success, and fulfillment.

Attracting Success with Positive Affirmations

We have a competitive world; success seems to be an elusive goal for many people. However, what if I told you that attracting success is not as complicated as it may seem? The key lies in harnessing Positive Affirmations. These simple yet incredibly powerful statements can transform your mindset, boost your confidence, and attract success into your life.

Positive affirmations are like seeds that you plant in the fertile soil of your subconscious mind. When nurtured consistently, they grow into a magnificent garden of success, happiness, and abundance. By repeating positive affirmations daily, you reprogram your mind, replacing negative thoughts and beliefs with empowering ones.

Affirmations for Life presents a collection of powerful affirmations specifically designed to attract success in all areas of your life. Whether you're seeking professional success, financial abundance, or personal growth, these affirmations will guide you towards your desired outcomes.

One of the fundamental principles of attracting success with positive affirmations is the law of attraction. This universal law states that like attracts like, meaning that your thoughts and beliefs shape the reality you experience. By practicing positive affirmations consistently, you align your thoughts with the success you desire, attracting it into your life.

Each affirmation in this subchapter has been carefully crafted to resonate with your subconscious mind and evoke a sense of confidence, determination, and self-belief. By repeating these affirmations daily, you will attract success and develop a positive mindset that will support you in overcoming challenges and setbacks.

Remember, success is not solely defined by external achievements, but also by inner growth and fulfillment. Affirmations for Life reminds you to focus on both aspects, encouraging you to cultivate self-love, gratitude, and resilience. When you believe in yourself and your abilities, success becomes an inevitable outcome.

So, if you're ready to transform your life and attract the success you deserve, dive into the pages of this subchapter. Embrace Positive Affirmations and watch as your life unfolds in ways you never thought possible. Get ready to attract success, live your dreams, and create a positive life filled with abundance and joy.

Chapter 5: Affirmations for Health and Well-Being

Nurturing Your Physical Body

In our fast-paced lives, it is easy to get caught up in the hustle and bustle, neglecting the most important aspect of our well-being – our physical body. Your body is your temple, and it requires nurturing and care to function at its best. In this subchapter, we will explore various ways to nurture your physical body and establish daily affirmations to support a positive and healthy lifestyle.

1. Embrace a Balanced Diet:

A well-balanced diet is the foundation of a healthy body. Nourish yourself with wholesome foods, incorporating various fruits, vegetables, whole grains, lean proteins, and healthy fats. Make conscious choices to avoid processed foods and sugary treats. Affirmation: "I choose to fuel my body with nutritious foods, providing it with the energy it needs to thrive."

2. Engage in Regular Exercise:

Physical activity is not only essential for maintaining a healthy weight but also for improving cardiovascular health, boosting mood, and enhancing overall well-being. Find activities that you enjoy, whether it's dancing, yoga, hiking, or swimming, and make them a regular part of your routine. Affirmation: "I honor my body by engaging in regular exercise, strengthening it and promoting vitality."

3. Prioritize Rest and Sleep:

Rest and sleep are vital for rejuvenation and allowing your body to repair and heal. Create a bedtime routine that promotes relaxation, such as reading a book, taking a warm bath, or practicing meditation. Ensure you get enough sleep each night to wake up feeling refreshed and ready for the day ahead. Affirmation: "I gift myself with restful sleep, granting my body the time it needs to restore and replenish."

4. Practice Mindful Self-Care:

Self-care goes beyond pampering yourself. It involves actively listening to your body's needs and responding with compassion. Take time for relaxation, practice deep breathing exercises, schedule regular massages or spa treatments, and engage in activities that bring you joy. Affirmation: "I honor my body by practicing mindful self-care, nurturing my physical and emotional well-being."

Conclusion:

Nurturing your physical body is an essential part of living a positive life. By embracing a balanced diet, engaging in regular exercise, prioritizing rest and sleep, and practicing mindful self-care, you can create a harmonious relationship with your body and enhance your overall well-being. The daily affirmations provided in this subchapter will serve as powerful reminders to support your journey towards a positive, healthy, and thriving life. Remember, your body is a precious gift, and by nurturing it, you can unlock your true potential and live life to the fullest.

Cultivating Mental and Emotional Wellness

Ours is a demanding world, it is more important than ever to prioritize our mental and emotional well-being. With the constant pressures and challenges we face, it is essential to develop effective strategies to nurture our minds and hearts. This subchapter, "Cultivating Mental and Emotional Wellness," explores Positive Affirmations in enhancing our overall well-being and offers practical guidance for integrating them into our daily lives.

Affirmations serve as positive statements that can rewire our thinking patterns and beliefs. By consciously repeating affirmations, we can redirect our thoughts towards positivity and create a more balanced and harmonious inner state. This practice allows us to cultivate mental and emotional resilience, enabling us to navigate life's ups and downs with grace and strength.

Talk Yourself Into Greatness lies in their ability to reprogram our subconscious mind. By consistently affirming positive statements, we can replace self-limiting beliefs with empowering ones. For example, repeating affirmations such as "I am worthy of love and happiness" or "I am capable of achieving my goals" can help us overcome self-doubt and build self-confidence. As we internalize these affirmations, they become our reality, transforming our lives from within.

This subchapter offers a range of affirmations specifically curated to support mental and emotional wellness. Whether you are seeking to reduce stress, boost self-esteem, or strengthen your relationships, these affirmations can be tailored to suit your unique needs. By incorporating them into your daily routine, you can create a positive and nurturing inner environment that supports your personal growth and well-being.

Furthermore, this subchapter provides guidance on how to effectively use affirmations. It highlights the importance of repetition, consistency, and belief in maximizing their impact. Additionally, it explores various techniques such as visualization and journaling to deepen the practice of affirmations and amplify their benefits.

Cultivating mental and emotional wellness is a lifelong journey, and affirmations are a powerful tool to support this process. By integrating them into your daily life, you can create a positive mindset, build emotional resilience, and experience a more fulfilling and joyful existence. Embrace the transformative power of affirmations and embark on a journey towards a positive and empowered life.

Enhancing Your Spiritual Connection

It's easy to get caught up in the daily grind and lose touch with our spiritual side. However, nurturing a strong spiritual connection is essential for finding inner peace, purpose, and living a fulfilling life. In this subchapter, we will explore various strategies and affirmations to help you deepen your spiritual connection.

1. Practice Mindfulness: Begin your journey towards enhancing your spiritual connection by practicing mindfulness. Take a few moments each day to be fully present in the moment, focusing on your breath and observing your thoughts without judgment. Mindfulness allows you to become more aware of your inner self and the world around you, fostering a deeper connection with your spirituality.

2. Engage in Meditation: Meditation is a powerful tool for enhancing your spiritual connection. Find a quiet space, close your eyes, and practice different meditation techniques such as visualization, loving-kindness, or mantra meditation. Regular meditation calms the mind and opens the door to spiritual growth and self-discovery.

3. Connect with Nature: Spending time in nature can be a profound way to enhance your spiritual connection. Take walks in the park, go hiking, or simply sit in your garden and observe the surrounding beauty. Nature has a way of grounding us and reminding us of our connection to something greater than ourselves.

4. Seek Spiritual Community: Surrounding yourself with like-minded individuals can provide support and encouragement on your spiritual journey. Seek spiritual communities, attend workshops or retreats, and engage in discussions with people who share similar beliefs. These connections can help you deepen your understanding, provide valuable insights, and create a sense of belonging.

5. Affirmations for Spiritual Growth: Affirmations are powerful statements that help reprogram your subconscious mind. Incorporating positive

affirmations into your daily routine can support your spiritual growth. Repeat affirmations such as "I am connected to a higher power," "I trust the divine guidance within me," or "I am open to receiving spiritual insights." These affirmations will help you align your thoughts and beliefs with your desire to enhance your spiritual connection.

By practicing mindfulness, engaging in meditation, connecting with nature, seeking spiritual community, and using affirmations for spiritual growth, you will find yourself on a path towards enhancing your spiritual connection. Remember, spirituality is a personal journey, and it's important to explore different practices until you find what resonates with you. Embrace this subchapter as an opportunity to delve deeper into your spiritual essence and experience a more fulfilling and purposeful life.

Promoting a Balanced Lifestyle

Achieving a balanced lifestyle is essential for our overall well-being and happiness. It involves consciously making choices that prioritize our physical, mental, and emotional health. In this subchapter, we will explore various affirmations and practices that can help you cultivate a balanced lifestyle and experience greater fulfillment in all areas of your life.

Physical well-being is the foundation of a balanced lifestyle. By taking care of our bodies through regular exercise, nourishing foods, and adequate rest, we can enhance our energy levels and improve our overall health. Repeat affirmations such as "I prioritize my physical health and make time for exercise and self-care" to reinforce your commitment to a healthy lifestyle. Incorporate activities you enjoy, such as yoga or dancing, into your routine to make it more enjoyable.

Mental and emotional balance is equally important. Affirmations such as "I choose to focus on positive thoughts and release negativity" can help shift your mindset and promote emotional well-being. Practice mindfulness and meditation to quiet your mind, reduce stress, and foster a sense of inner peace. Create a gratitude journal to remind yourself of the blessings in your life and cultivate a positive outlook.

Balancing work and personal life is a common challenge in today's fast-paced world. Affirmations like "I create boundaries to maintain a healthy work-life balance" can help you prioritize your personal time and relationships. Make time for activities that rejuvenate you, such as hobbies, spending time with loved ones, or pursuing personal goals. Establishing clear boundaries between work and personal life will help you maintain a sense of balance and prevent burnout.

Remember, achieving a balanced lifestyle is a continuous journey. It requires making conscious choices and regularly reassessing your priorities. Experiment with different practices and affirmations to find what works best for you. By promoting a balanced lifestyle, you will experience increased happiness, improved relationships, and a greater sense of fulfillment in all aspects of your life.

Incorporate these affirmations and practices into your daily routine and watch as your life transforms into a harmonious and fulfilling journey towards a balanced lifestyle.

Chapter 6: Affirmations for Relationships and Connection

Cultivating Healthy and Supportive Relationships

In our journey towards a positive and fulfilling life, one of the most crucial aspects is the relationships we build and nurture. Our connections with others have a profound impact on our overall well-being and success. Therefore, it is essential to focus on cultivating healthy and supportive relationships in our lives.

The first step towards fostering healthy relationships is to start with ourselves. Self-love and self-care are the foundations upon which we build all other relationships. By practicing daily affirmations that reinforce our worth and value, we empower ourselves to attract and maintain healthy connections. Affirmations such as, "I deserve love and respect," or "I am a magnet for positive and supportive relationships," can help instill a sense of self-worth and attract like-minded individuals into our lives.

Once we have established a strong sense of self, it is important to surround ourselves'with people who uplift and support us. Negative and toxic relationships can drain our energy and hinder our progress towards a positive life. By setting boundaries and recognizing red flags, we can distance ourselves from toxic individuals and create space for healthy connections to flourish.

Communication is the cornerstone of any successful relationship. Open and honest communication allows for understanding, empathy, and growth. By practicing affirmations such as, "I communicate my needs and desires effectively," or "I listen with compassion and understanding," we promote healthy dialogue and build trust with our loved ones.

Forgiveness is another vital aspect of cultivating healthy relationships. Holding on to grudges and resentments only serves to poison our connections. By affirming statements like, "I release all bitterness and forgive those who have hurt me," we free ourselves from the burden of past pain and create space for healing and growth within our relationships.

It is essential to express gratitude and appreciation for the people in our lives. Acknowledging the positive aspects of our relationships and expressing gratitude fosters a sense of connection and strengthens the bond between individuals. By practicing affirmations like, "I am grateful for the love and support in my life," or "I appreciate the kindness and understanding of my loved ones," we invite more love and positivity into our relationships.

Considering what we do know, cultivating healthy and supportive relationships is vital for our overall well-being and success. By starting with self-love, setting boundaries, practicing effective communication, embracing forgiveness, and expressing gratitude, we can build and nurture the connections that bring joy and fulfillment into our lives. Remember, affirmations are powerful tools that can help us transform our relationships and create a positive and supportive environment for ourselves and those around us.

Enhancing Communication and Understanding

In our interconnected world, effective communication and understanding have become essential skills for navigating through life. Whether it is in our personal relationships, professional endeavors, or simply in our day-to-day interactions with others, the ability to communicate clearly and understand one another is crucial for living a positive life.

Communication is not just about the words we speak, but also about how we listen and respond. It is a two-way street that requires active participation from both parties involved. By enhancing our communication skills, we can foster better connections, resolve conflicts, and build stronger relationships.

One powerful tool we can utilize to enhance communication and understanding is affirmations. Affirmations are positive statements that we repeat to ourselves to reprogram our subconscious mind. By incorporating affirmations into our daily lives, we can transform our thought patterns and beliefs, and ultimately elevate our communication skills.

For instance, we can affirm statements such as "I am an excellent communicator" or "I listen attentively and respond with empathy." By repeating these affirmations daily, we can instill confidence in our ability to communicate effectively, and in turn, enhance our understanding of others.

Furthermore, practicing active listening is another vital aspect of enhancing communication and understanding. Active listening involves giving our full attention to the speaker, maintaining eye contact, and being fully present in the conversation. By doing so, we create a safe and open space for the speaker to express themselves, leading to a more in-depth understanding between individuals.

Additionally, it is important to be mindful of our non-verbal communication cues. Our body language, facial expressions, and tone of voice can greatly influence how our message is received. By being aware of these non-verbal cues and ensuring they align with our words, we can enhance the clarity and effectiveness of our communication.

Fostering empathy and understanding towards others plays a significant role in enhancing communication. By putting ourselves in someone else's shoes and seeking to understand their perspective, we can break down barriers and build stronger connections. Affirmations such as "I am compassionate and understanding" can help cultivate empathy within us and promote more meaningful interactions with others.

All in all, enhancing communication and understanding is an ongoing process that requires conscious effort and practice. By incorporating daily affirmations, practicing active listening, being mindful of non-verbal cues, and fostering empathy, we can elevate our communication skills and create more positive and fulfilling relationships in all areas of life.

Opening Your Heart to Love and Vulnerability

Love is a powerful force that has the ability to transform our lives in ways we could never imagine. It can heal wounds, ignite passions, and bring us immense joy. However, love also requires vulnerability – the willingness to open our hearts and expose ourselves to the possibility of hurt and disappointment. In this subchapter, we will explore the importance of opening your heart to love and vulnerability, and how affirmations can help you navigate this beautiful yet challenging journey.

For many people, the fear of getting hurt or rejected can often lead to a guarded heart. We build walls around ourselves, shielding us from potential pain. But what we fail to realize is that by closing ourselves off, we also block out the possibility of experiencing deep connections and genuine love. Affirmations can help you break down those walls, allowing love to flow freely into your life.

Repeat affirmations such as, "I am worthy of love and happiness," or "I embrace vulnerability and allow love to enter my life." These positive statements will gradually rewire your subconscious mind, replacing limiting beliefs with empowering thoughts. As you affirm your worthiness of love, you will begin to attract loving and fulfilling relationships into your life.

Opening your heart to vulnerability does not mean disregarding your boundaries or putting yourself in harm's way. It means being willing to take emotional risks and allowing yourself to be seen and loved for whom you truly are. Affirmations like, "I trust in the process of love," or "I am safe and supported in all my relationships," will help alleviate any fears or doubts that may arise.

Remember, vulnerability is not a sign of weakness, but a testament to your strength. By allowing yourself to be vulnerable, you create the space for authentic connections and profound growth. Affirmations can act as a gentle reminder to embrace vulnerability and let love in.

In essence, opening your heart to love and vulnerability is an essential aspect of living a positive and fulfilling life. Affirmations can serve as powerful tools in this journey, helping you release fears, build self-worth, and attract healthy relationships. Embrace vulnerability, trust in the process, and watch as love flows effortlessly into your life.

Fostering Connection in a Digital Age

Fostering genuine connections has become a challenge. We find ourselves constantly glued to our devices, seeking validation and connection in the virtual realm. But amidst this digital chaos, it is essential to remember the importance of fostering real connections that nourish our souls and bring us true happiness.

In this subchapter, we explore the significance of fostering connection in a digital age and provide practical affirmations for people seeking to cultivate meaningful relationships in their lives.

1. Disconnect to Connect: In a world where our devices have become an extension of ourselves, it is crucial to disconnect from technology and be fully present with the people around us. By setting aside dedicated time to engage in face-to-face interactions, we can build deeper connections and truly understand one another.

Affirmation: "I am present in the moment and actively engage in meaningful conversations, fostering deep connections with those around me."

2. Authenticity over Perfection: In an era driven by curated online personas, it's easy to get caught up in portraying a perfect image. However, true connections are built on authenticity and vulnerability. Embrace your imperfections and allow others to see the real you, fostering genuine connections that withstand the test of time.

Affirmation: "I embrace my authentic self, allowing genuine connections to flourish in my life."

3. Active Listening: In a digital age filled with distractions, active listening has become a lost art.

To foster genuine connections, it is crucial to practice active listening – giving our undivided attention, empathizing, and truly understanding others. By doing so, we create a safe space for open communication and strengthen our relationships.

Affirmation: "I am a compassionate listener, creating a space for others to express themselves fully and fostering deeper connections."

4. Cultivate Empathy: Empathy lies at the heart of meaningful connections. In a society increasingly disconnected from the emotions and experiences of others, cultivating empathy is essential. By putting ourselves in others' shoes, seeking to understand their perspectives, and offering support, we foster connections built on compassion and understanding.

Affirmation: "I cultivate empathy, understanding the experiences of others and nurturing connections based on compassion."

In sum, in this digital age, fostering genuine connections has become more important than ever. By disconnecting from technology, embracing our authentic selves, actively listening, and cultivating empathy, we can create a space for meaningful connections to thrive. Let us remember that true happiness lies not in the number of online connections but in the quality of the relationships we nurture offline.

Chapter 7: Affirmations for Abundance and Prosperity

Shifting Your Mindset towards Abundance

It's easy to get caught up in a scarcity mindset. We constantly worry about not having enough – not enough money, not enough time, not enough success. But what if we told you that there is a way to break free from this limited thinking and embrace a mindset of abundance? Welcome to the subchapter on "Shifting Your Mindset towards Abundance" from the book "Daily Affirmations for a Positive Life."

Dear people, we understand that life can often feel like a never-ending struggle, but it doesn't have to be that way. By shifting your mindset towards abundance, you can transform your life in remarkable ways. But how do you do that?

First and foremost, it's crucial to recognize that abundance is not just about material possessions. It goes beyond money and possessions; it encompasses all aspects of life – love, happiness, health, and opportunities. Abundance is a state of mind, and it starts with changing your perspective.

One powerful tool to help you shift your mindset is affirmations. Affirmations for life are positive statements that you can repeat to yourself daily, reminding you of the abundant possibilities that exist in your life. By consistently reciting affirmations, you rewire your brain to focus on the positives, attracting more abundance into your life.

Begin by acknowledging the abundance that already exists in your life. Take a moment each day to appreciate the blessings you have – your supportive relationships, your health, your talents, and the opportunities that come your way. Expressing gratitude for what you have opens the door for more abundance to flow into your life.

Next, release any limiting beliefs that may be holding you back. Often, we are our worst enemies, allowing negative thoughts and self-doubt to sabotage our potential for abundance. Challenge these beliefs and replace them with positive, empowering thoughts. Visualize the life of abundance you desire, and believe that it is within your reach.

Additionally, surround yourself with people who uplift and inspire you. Choose friends and mentors who have a positive mindset and a prosperity consciousness. Their energy and perspective will support and reinforce your shift towards abundance.

Remember, shifting your mindset towards abundance is a continuous practice. It requires patience, persistence, and a willingness to let go of scarcity thinking. By adopting a mindset of abundance, you open yourself up to a world of endless possibilities. Embrace Positive Affirmations, gratitude, positive beliefs, and supportive relationships, and watch as your life transforms into a truly abundant and fulfilling experience.

So, let us embark on this journey together, embracing abundance as our birthright and creating a positive life filled with joy, love, and prosperity.

Embracing a Wealth Consciousness

In today's fast-paced world, the pursuit of wealth has become a significant aspect of our lives. However, many people find themselves struggling to attain financial success, feeling trapped in a cycle of lack and scarcity. The key to breaking free from this mindset lies in embracing a wealth consciousness.

A wealth consciousness is a state of mind that allows individuals to recognize and attract abundance into their lives. It involves developing a positive perception of money and understanding that wealth is not merely about material possessions but rather a tool for personal growth and fulfillment.

To cultivate a wealth consciousness, one must start by shifting their mindset. Affirmations play a crucial role in this process. By repeating positive statements about wealth and abundance, individuals can reprogram their subconscious minds, allowing them to believe in their ability to create wealth and attract prosperity.

Affirmations for life can be a powerful tool in developing a wealth consciousness. By repeating affirmations such as "I am worthy of abundance," "Money flows easily and effortlessly into my life," or "I have the power to create unlimited wealth," individuals open themselves up to the infinite possibilities that exist in the universe.

Additionally, it is vital to surround oneself with positive influences and like-minded individuals who share a similar mindset. Engaging with communities or groups focused on wealth creation can provide support, motivation, and valuable insights into achieving financial success.

Furthermore, embracing a wealth consciousness requires taking inspired action. It is not enough to merely repeat affirmations without taking steps towards financial empowerment. Setting clear goals, creating a financial plan, and seeking opportunities for growth and investment are all crucial components of this journey.

It is important to remember that wealth consciousness is not solely about personal gain. It also involves giving back and making a positive impact on others' lives. Recognizing the power of wealth to create change and using it responsibly can lead to a deeper sense of fulfillment and purpose.

As a result, embracing a wealth consciousness is a transformative journey that allows individuals to break free from limiting beliefs and attract abundance into their lives. By shifting their mindset, repeating affirmations, surrounding themselves with positive influences, and taking inspired action, people can create a life of financial freedom, personal growth, and meaningful contribution.

Attracting Financial Prosperity

In today's fast-paced world, where financial stability and prosperity are highly sought after, it is essential to harness the power of positive thinking and affirmations to manifest abundance in our lives. This subchapter, "Attracting Financial Prosperity," aims to guide and inspire people from all walks of life to cultivate a mindset of abundance and attract financial success.

It is a widely recognized fact that our thoughts shape our reality. By harnessing Positive Affirmations, we can rewire our minds to focus on abundance, wealth, and financial prosperity. Affirmations are positive statements that, when repeated regularly, help to reprogram our subconscious mind and align our thoughts with our desires. They serve as a powerful tool to shift our mindset from lack to abundance.

In this subchapter, we will explore a range of affirmations specifically designed to attract financial prosperity. These affirmations will empower readers to let go of limiting beliefs around money and embrace a mindset of abundance. Through the power of repetition and belief, readers will learn to attract and manifest the financial success they desire.

The affirmations in this subchapter will cover various aspects of financial prosperity, including abundance, wealth, success, and the law of attraction. Readers will discover how to affirm their worthiness of financial abundance, release any fears or doubts around money, and embrace a mindset of gratitude and prosperity. By consistently practicing these affirmations, readers will open themselves up to receiving wealth and financial opportunities in their lives.

Furthermore, this subchapter will also provide practical tips and strategies to complement the affirmations. These tips will include suggestions on creating a vision board, setting financial goals, and taking inspired action towards achieving financial prosperity.

"Attracting Financial Prosperity" is a valuable resource for individuals seeking to improve their financial situation and create a positive mindset around money. By implementing the affirmations and strategies outlined in this subchapter, readers will be equipped with the tools necessary to attract financial abundance and experience a positive transformation in their lives.

Remember, financial prosperity is not just about the money; it is about creating a life of freedom, security, and abundance. With Positive Affirmations and a mindset of abundance, you can attract the financial success you deserve. So, dive into this subchapter, embrace the affirmations, and watch as your financial reality transforms before your eyes.

Gratitude and Appreciation for Abundance

In our fast-paced lives, it is easy to get caught up in the frenzy of chasing success, wealth, and material possessions. We often forget to pause and express gratitude for the abundance that already exists in our lives. This subchapter, titled "Gratitude and Appreciation for Abundance," is dedicated to helping you cultivate a mindset of appreciation and amplify the positive energy that flows through your life.

Gratitude is a powerful tool that can transform your life in remarkable ways. When you shift your focus towards gratitude, you begin to notice the countless blessings that surround you each day. From the smallest gestures of kindness to the grand achievements, expressing appreciation opens the door to receiving more abundance in your life.

This subchapter will guide you through a series of affirmations that will help you tap into the limitless potential of gratitude. These daily affirmations will serve as a reminder to acknowledge and appreciate the abundance that already exists within and around you. By practicing these affirmations, you will gradually rewire your mind to see the world through a lens of gratitude, thus attracting more positivity and abundance into your life.

Affirmations for Life is a niche that focuses on empowering individuals to create a positive mindset and manifest their dreams. In this subchapter, we will explore affirmations that specifically address gratitude and appreciation for abundance. These affirmations will help you cultivate a deep sense of appreciation for the present moment, the people in your life, and the opportunities that come your way.

By regularly practicing these affirmations, you will begin to experience a profound shift in your perspective. You will find yourself noticing the beauty in the simplest things, feeling more connected to others, and attracting more abundance into your life. With each affirmation, you will be reminded of the abundance that already exists within you, unlocking the potential for limitless growth and fulfillment.

Whether you are just starting your journey of self-discovery or are already on a path of personal growth, this subchapter will provide you with the tools and inspiration to embrace gratitude and appreciation for abundance. Get ready to open your heart and mind to the infinite possibilities that await you as you embark on this transformative journey towards a positive and abundant life.

Chapter 8: Affirmations for Personal Growth and Transformation

Embracing Change and Transformation

Change is an inevitable part of life. It is the only constant that we can truly rely on. Yet, many of us struggle to embrace change and find ourselves resisting it, clinging to outdated beliefs and patterns that no longer serve us. To live a positive and fulfilling life, we must learn to embrace change and allow ourselves to transform.

Change can be intimidating and can bring about feelings of uncertainty and fear. However, it is important to remember that change is not always negative. In fact, it often presents opportunities for growth and personal development. By embracing change, we open ourselves up to new possibilities, experiences, and perspectives that can enrich our lives in ways we never imagined.

One powerful tool that can support us in embracing change and transformation is affirmations. Affirmations are positive statements that can help us shift our mindset, beliefs, and behaviors. By repeating affirmations daily, we can reprogram our subconscious mind and align ourselves with the positive changes we want to manifest in our lives.

Here are some affirmations for embracing change and transformation:

1. "I embrace change with an open heart and mind, knowing that it brings new opportunities for growth."

2. "I am adaptable and flexible, easily adjusting to the changes that come my way."

3. "I trust that change is leading me towards a better version of myself and a more fulfilling life."

4. "I release resistance and allow change to flow through me, knowing that it serves my highest good."

5. "I am grateful for the lessons that change brings, as they help me evolve and become the best version of myself."

6. "I am a magnet for positive transformation, attracting the people, circumstances, and experiences that support my growth."

7. "I let go of the past and embrace the present moment, allowing change to shape my future."

By incorporating these affirmations into your daily routine, you can begin to shift your mindset and open yourself up to the transformative power of change. Remember, change is not something to be feared, but rather an opportunity for personal growth and a chance to create a positive and fulfilling life. Embrace change and watch as your life transforms in ways you never thought possible.

Releasing Limiting Beliefs

In our journey towards a positive and fulfilling life, one of the most difficult obstacles we often encounter are our own limiting beliefs. These beliefs, typically deeply ingrained in our subconscious mind, can hold us back from realizing our true potential and living the life we desire. However, by recognizing and releasing these limiting beliefs, we can pave the way for a more positive and empowering mindset.

Limiting beliefs can manifest in various areas of our lives, such as relationships, career, and personal growth. They stem from experiences, societal conditioning, and negative self-talk. For example, a person may believe they are not worthy of love and affection due to a past heartbreak or repeatedly being told they are unlovable. This belief can create a self-fulfilling prophecy, leading to a cycle of failed relationships and emotional pain.

To release these limiting beliefs, we must first identify them. This requires introspection and self-awareness. Take some time to reflect on the areas of your life where you feel stuck or experience recurring negative patterns. What thoughts or beliefs come to mind when you think about those areas? Write them down and examine them objectively.

Once you have identified your limiting beliefs, it's time to challenge them. Ask yourself if these beliefs are based on facts or merely assumptions. Are they helping or hindering your personal growth? Often, we discover that these beliefs are outdated and no longer serve us.

To replace these limiting beliefs with empowering ones, affirmations play a crucial role. Affirmations are positive statements that help rewire our subconscious mind. For example, if your limiting belief is "I am not smart enough to succeed," replace it with "I am intelligent and capable of achieving my goals." Repeat these affirmations daily, preferably in front of a mirror, and truly believe in their power to transform your mindset.

Additionally, surround yourself with positive influences and supportive individuals. Seek motivational books, podcasts, and communities that uplift and inspire you. Engage in activities that boost your self-confidence and challenge your old beliefs. Remember, you have the power to rewrite your story.

Releasing limiting beliefs is an ongoing process. It requires patience, persistence, and self-compassion. As you continue to challenge and replace these beliefs, you will notice a shift in your mindset and actions. Embrace the journey of personal growth, and trust that by releasing your limiting beliefs, you are creating space for a more positive and fulfilling life.

Cultivating a Growth Mindset

In this ever-changing world, it is crucial to develop a growth mindset that allows us to embrace challenges, learn from failures, and continuously improve ourselves. This subchapter titled "Cultivating a Growth Mindset" in the book "Daily Affirmations for a Positive Life" aims to inspire and empower people in the niche of "Affirmations for Life" to adopt a growth mindset and unlock their full potential.

A growth mindset is the belief that our abilities and intelligence can be developed through dedication, effort, and perseverance. It encourages us to view obstacles as opportunities for growth and see failures as stepping stones towards success. By cultivating a growth mindset, we can overcome self-limiting beliefs, strengthen our resilience, and achieve personal and professional growth.

This subchapter begins by explaining the concept of a growth mindset and how it differs from a fixed mindset. It emphasizes that our mindset determines our attitude towards challenges, failures, and our ability to learn and grow. It highlights the importance of embracing a growth mindset to lead a fulfilling and successful life.

The content then explores practical strategies and techniques to develop and nurture a growth mindset. It provides daily affirmations and exercises that help individuals change their self-talk, challenge negative beliefs, and develop a positive and growth-oriented mindset. It encourages readers to embrace mistakes, seek feedback, and continuously learn and improve.

Furthermore, the subchapter delves into the benefits of a growth mindset. It explains how a growth mindset enhances creativity, resilience, and adaptability, and enables individuals to overcome obstacles and achieve their goals. It also emphasizes the impact of a growth mindset on personal relationships and success in various domains of life.

To reinforce the message and engage the audience, real-life examples and success stories are shared throughout the subchapter. These stories illustrate how individuals with a growth mindset transformed their lives, achieved personal and professional milestones, and overcame seemingly insurmountable challenges.

Overall, "Cultivating a Growth Mindset" is an empowering subchapter that encourages people in the niche of "Affirmations for Life" to adopt a growth mindset and unlock their full potential. By providing practical strategies, daily affirmations, and real-life examples, this subchapter inspires readers to embrace challenges, learn from failures, and continuously grow and improve themselves.

Stepping into Your Authentic Self

In our journey towards self-discovery and personal growth, one of the most rewarding experiences is stepping into our authentic selves. This subchapter aims to guide you on this transformative path, providing insights and affirmations to help you embrace your true essence and live a positive, fulfilling life.

Authenticity is about being true to ourselves, honoring our values, and aligning our actions with our innermost desires. It requires an in-depth understanding of who we are and what brings us joy, as well as the courage to let go of societal expectations and judgments.

To begin this empowering journey, it is crucial to cultivate self-awareness. Take time each day to connect with your inner self through meditation, journaling, or simply spending quiet moments in introspection. By listening to your heart and acknowledging your feelings, you can start uncovering your authentic desires and passions.

Once you have gained a more in-depth understanding of yourself, it's time to align your thoughts and actions with your authentic self. Affirmations play a powerful role in this process. By repeating positive statements that reflect your true nature, you can rewire your subconscious mind and bring about positive change in your life.

Here are a few affirmations to help you step into your authentic self:

1. I embrace my uniqueness and let go of the need for approval from others.

2. I trust my intuition and make choices that align with my authentic desires.

3. I release the fear of judgment and fully express my true self.

4. I am worthy of love and acceptance just as I am.

5. I confidently pursue my passions and create a life that resonates with my authentic self.

Remember, stepping into your authentic self is an ongoing process. It requires self-reflection, self-compassion, and the willingness to grow. Embrace the journey with an open heart and mind, and allow yourself to evolve into the best version of yourself.

Note that, stepping into your authentic self is a powerful and transformative experience. By cultivating self-awareness, aligning your thoughts and actions, and embracing affirmations that reflect your true nature, you can unlock your full potential and create a positive, fulfilling life. Embrace your uniqueness, trust yourself, and release the fear of judgment. Step by step, you will find yourself living a life that resonates with your authentic self, bringing you joy, fulfillment, and a deep sense of purpose.

Chapter 9: Affirmations for Inner Peace and Happiness

Finding Inner Peace in a Chaotic World

Living in a chaotic world, finding inner peace can seem like an impossible task. We often find ourselves overwhelmed by work, relationships, and the constant barrage of information from technology. However, it is crucial to prioritize our mental well-being and strive for inner peace amidst the chaos.

Inner peace is a state of mind that allows us to feel calm, centered, and content, regardless of external circumstances. It is not about escaping reality or avoiding challenges, but rather cultivating a sense of tranquility and balance within ourselves. By incorporating daily affirmations into our lives, we can gradually train our minds to find peace and embrace the positive aspects of life.

Affirmations are powerful tools that can shift our mindset and help us overcome negative thought patterns. They are positive statements that we repeat to ourselves to reinforce desired beliefs and behaviors. By using affirmations, we can rewire our brains to focus on the present moment, let go of worries, and find peace within ourselves.

One powerful affirmation to incorporate into your daily routine is, "I am deserving of inner peace, and I choose to cultivate it every day." Remind yourself that inner peace is your birthright, and you have the power to invite it into your life. Repeat this affirmation each morning and throughout the day, especially during moments of stress or anxiety.

Another helpful affirmation is, "I release all negative thoughts and emotions, allowing peace to flow through me." Recognize that holding onto negative thoughts only perpetuates chaos and prevents you from experiencing true peace. Let go of anger, frustration, and resentment, and make room for positivity and serenity to enter your life.

Furthermore, practice mindfulness and meditation to connect with your inner self and find tranquility. Set aside a few minutes each day to sit in silence, focus on your breath, and detach from the noise of the outside world. This simple practice can bring immense peace and clarity to your mind.

Remember, finding inner peace is a lifelong journey, and it requires consistent effort and self-reflection. Embrace the power of daily affirmations and make them a part of your routine. With time and practice, you will find the strength and resilience to navigate the chaos of the world while remaining centered and at peace within yourself.

Letting Go of Negativity and Stress

It's easy to get caught up in the whirlwind of negativity and stress. From demanding work schedules to personal challenges and societal pressures, it can sometimes feel overwhelming. However, it is essential to remember that we have the power to let go of these burdens and create a positive life filled with joy and contentment.

Negativity and stress can drain our energy, affect our mental and physical health, and hinder our ability to achieve our goals. We need to recognize that we have the power to change our mindset and let go of these toxic emotions. By consciously choosing to release negativity and stress, we open ourselves up to a world of possibilities and create space for positive experiences.

One effective way to let go of negativity and stress is through daily affirmations. Affirmations are powerful statements that help rewire our thought patterns and shape our reality. By repeating positive and empowering affirmations daily, we can reprogram our subconscious mind and cultivate a more positive outlook on life.

Affirmations for Life are a collection of uplifting and inspiring affirmations specifically designed to help people let go of negativity and stress. Within this subchapter, you will find a treasure trove of affirmations that will guide you towards a more positive and stress-free life.

By practicing these affirmations consistently, you will begin to notice a shift in your mindset. Negative thoughts will lose their power, and stress will no longer hold you captive. Instead, you will embrace a more optimistic perspective, attracting positive experiences and opportunities into your life.

In addition to affirmations, this subchapter also provides practical tips and techniques to help you release negativity and stress. From mindfulness exercises to gratitude practices, you will discover a wide range of tools that can support your journey towards a more positive life.

Remember, letting go of negativity and stress is a continuous practice. It requires self-awareness, patience, and dedication. By incorporating the affirmations and techniques shared in this subchapter into your daily routine, you will gradually transform your life and create a more positive and fulfilling existence.

Embrace the power within you to let go of negativity and stress. Start your journey towards a positive life today and watch as Joy, peace, and abundance flow effortlessly into your world.

Cultivating Joy and Gratitude

It can be easy to lose sight of the simple pleasures in life. We get caught up in the daily grind, focusing on our to-do lists and never-ending responsibilities. However, it is essential to take a step back and remind ourselves of the importance of cultivating joy and gratitude in our lives.

Joy is a powerful emotion that can uplift our spirits, increase our overall well-being, and expand our relationships with others. By intentionally seeking moments of joy, we can create a positive ripple effect that impacts every aspect of our lives. Whether it's finding joy in the small things, such as a beautiful sunset or a cup of warm coffee, or engaging in activities that bring us pure delight, like dancing or singing. It is crucial to prioritize joy in our daily lives.

Gratitude, on the other hand, is a mindset that allows us to appreciate and acknowledge the blessings and abundance in our lives. When we shift our focus from what we lack to what we have, we open ourselves up to a world of possibilities and contentment. By practicing gratitude regularly, we can train our minds to see the positive aspects of our lives, even during challenging times.

This subchapter explores various strategies and affirmations that can help people cultivate joy and gratitude in their lives. It provides practical exercises, such as keeping a gratitude journal, practicing mindfulness, and engaging in acts of kindness. These activities not only help individuals develop a more positive outlook but also foster a sense of connectedness with others and the world around them.

Furthermore, this subchapter also delves into Talk Yourself Into Greatness for cultivating joy and gratitude. Affirmations are positive statements that we repeat to ourselves regularly to reinforce positive beliefs and attitudes. By incorporating affirmations into our daily routine, we can rewire our brains to focus on the good, boost our self-confidence, and attract more positive experiences into our lives.

After all, cultivating joy and gratitude is a transformative practice that can enhance our overall well-being and outlook on life. This subchapter provides practical tools, exercises, and affirmations for people seeking to infuse their lives with more joy and gratitude. By incorporating these practices into our daily routines, we can live a more positive and fulfilling life, appreciating the beauty and blessings that surround us.

Creating a Life of Happiness and Fulfillment

In this fast-paced and often chaotic world, it can be easy to get caught up in the daily grind and lose sight of what truly brings us happiness and fulfillment. However, with a little intention and effort, it is possible to create a life that is filled with joy, purpose, and contentment. This subchapter will explore various strategies and affirmations that will guide you towards living a life of happiness and fulfillment.

One of the first steps towards creating a happy and fulfilling life is to identify what brings you joy and fulfillment. This could be pursuing a passion, spending time with loved ones, or engaging in activities that align with your values. Take some time to reflect on what truly makes you happy and create a list of these things. By actively incorporating them into your life, you will be laying the foundation for a life filled with joy and contentment.

Another important aspect of creating a fulfilling life is to cultivate a positive mindset. Affirmations play a crucial role in this process. Affirmations are positive statements that you repeat to yourself regularly to reinforce positive beliefs and attitudes. By incorporating affirmations into your daily routine, you can shift your mindset towards positivity and abundance. For example, you can affirm statements such as "I am deserving of happiness and fulfillment," "I attract positivity and joy into my life," or "I am grateful for all the blessings in my life." Repeat these affirmations daily and truly believe in their power to manifest your desired reality.

Additionally, surrounding yourself with positive influences and supportive people is essential for creating a life of happiness and fulfillment. Seek individuals who uplift and inspire you, and distance yourself from those who bring negativity or drain your energy. By surrounding yourself with positivity, you will be better equipped to maintain a positive mindset and attract happiness and fulfillment into your life.

Remember that creating a life of happiness and fulfillment is an ongoing journey. It requires consistent effort, self-reflection, and a commitment to prioritizing your well-being. By implementing the strategies and affirmations outlined in this subchapter, you will be well on your way towards living a life filled with joy, purpose, and contentment. Embrace the power of positive thinking and watch as your life transforms into the fulfilling and happy existence you deserve.

Chapter 10: Affirmations for Daily Practice and Integration

Creating a Daily Affirmation Routine

In our fast-paced and often stressful lives, it is crucial to nourish our minds with positivity and cultivate a mindset for success and happiness. Daily affirmations are a powerful tool that can transform our lives and help us achieve our goals. By incorporating a daily affirmation routine into our lives, we can rewire our brains to focus on the positive, overcome self-doubt, and manifest our deepest desires.

To begin your affirmation journey, it is essential to set aside a specific time each day to focus on your affirmations. Whether it's in the morning when you wake up or before you go to bed, find a time that works best for you. Consistency is key here, so make it a non-negotiable part of your routine.

Start by selecting affirmations that resonate with you on a deep level. Affirmations are positive statements that reflect your desires and goals. For example, if you want to enhance your self-confidence, you might choose an affirmation such as, "I am confident and capable of achieving anything I set my mind to." Write down your affirmations in a journal or create a digital affirmation board, ensuring they are visible and easily accessible.

Once you have your affirmations, repeat them to yourself out loud or silently. Engage all your senses and truly believe in the words you are saying. Visualization is a powerful technique that can amplify the effects of affirmations. When repeating your affirmations, imagine yourself already living the life you desire, feeling the emotions associated with your goals.

To make your daily affirmation routine even more effective, consider incorporating additional practices. Meditation, deep breathing exercises, or visualization can help calm your mind and connect with your affirmations on a deeper level. Journaling is another valuable tool to reflect on your progress, jot down any limiting beliefs that arise, and reframe them with positive affirmations.

Remember, creating a daily affirmation routine is a journey, and consistency is essential. As you repeat your affirmations daily, you will notice subtle shifts in your mindset and behavior. Over time, these shifts will lead to significant positive changes in your life.

So, take the first step today. Start by setting aside time each day to focus on your affirmations. Choose affirmations that resonate with you, repeat them with conviction, and visualize the life you desire. With dedication and persistence, you will unlock the power of daily affirmations and create a positive, fulfilling life.

Incorporating Affirmations into Your Morning Ritual

Talk Yourself Into Greatness is undeniable. These simple yet profound statements can transform our thoughts, beliefs, and actions, leading us towards a more positive and fulfilling life. And what better way to harness their power than by incorporating affirmations into our morning ritual? By starting our day with positive intentions and affirmations, we can set the tone for a day filled with positivity, productivity, and success.

So, how can we effectively incorporate affirmations into our morning routine?

Firstly, it is crucial to create a peaceful and conducive environment for your morning ritual. Find a quiet space where you can be alone with your thoughts, free from any distractions. This could be a cozy corner in your bedroom or a serene spot in your garden. Make it your personal sanctuary, where you can connect with yourself and your affirmations.

Next, take a few deep breaths and center yourself. Close your eyes and visualize the life you desire. What are your goals, dreams, and aspirations? How do you want to feel today? Choose affirmations that align with your intentions and write them down. For example, if you want to cultivate self-confidence, your affirmation could be: "I am confident and capable of achieving anything I set my mind to."

Once you have your affirmations, it's time to bring them to life. Speak them out loud with conviction and belief. Repeat them several times, allowing their positive energy to permeate your being. Feel the words resonate within you, and let them uplift and empower you.

To enhance the effectiveness of your affirmations, pair them with visualization. As you repeat your affirmations, visualize yourself living them in your mind's eye. See yourself confidently acing that presentation, or achieving your fitness goals. Engage all your senses to make the visualization more vivid and impactful.

Lastly, carry the energy of your affirmations throughout your day. Let them guide your thoughts, decisions, and actions. Whenever you face challenges or negative thoughts, recall your affirmations and repeat them silently to yourself. By doing so, you reinforce positive beliefs and attract the outcomes you desire.

Remember, incorporating affirmations into your morning ritual is a powerful practice that can transform your life. By starting each day with positive intentions and affirmations, you create a solid foundation for success, happiness, and fulfillment. So, make it a daily habit, and embrace Positive Affirmations in your life!

Using Affirmations throughout Your Day

In today's fast-paced world, it's easy to get overwhelmed by negative thoughts and emotions.

However, by incorporating affirmations into your daily routine, you can transform your mindset and create a positive life. Affirmations are simple yet powerful statements that can help you rewire your brain and shift your focus towards the good things in life.

Begin each day with affirmations to set the tone for positivity and success. As soon as you wake up, take a few moments to repeat affirmations that resonate with you. Speak them out loud or silently to yourself, allowing their words to sink deep into your subconscious mind. By starting your day with positive affirmations, you are priming your mind for a day filled with abundance and joy.

Throughout the day, take advantage of every opportunity to use affirmations. When faced with challenges or negative thoughts, counteract them with positive affirmations. For example, if you find yourself doubting your abilities, repeat affirmations such as "I am capable and confident in everything I do" or "I embrace challenges as opportunities for growth." By doing so, you are reminding yourself of your inherent strengths and shifting your focus towards solutions rather than problems.

Incorporating affirmations into your daily routine can also be done through visualization. Close your eyes and visualize yourself living your best life, achieving your goals, and experiencing happiness. As you visualize, repeat affirmations that align with your desired outcome. This powerful combination of visualizing and affirming can help manifest your dreams into reality.

Furthermore, affirmations can be used as a tool to combat stress and anxiety. When you feel overwhelmed, take a moment to breathe deeply and repeat affirmations that promote calmness and relaxation. For instance, say to yourself, "I am at peace" or "I release all tension and embrace tranquility." By doing this, you are training your mind to let go of stress and embrace a state of calmness.

In essence, incorporating affirmations into your daily life can have a profound impact on your overall well-being. By starting your day with affirmations, countering negativity with positive statements, visualizing your desired outcomes, and using affirmations to combat stress, you can create a positive life filled with abundance and joy. So, embrace Positive Affirmations and watch as your life transforms for the better.

Reflecting and Reviewing Your Affirmation Practice

In the journey of self-improvement and personal growth, affirmations play a vital role in shaping our thoughts, beliefs, and actions. They are powerful tools that can help us overcome challenges, cultivate a positive mindset, and manifest the life we desire. As you continue to incorporate affirmations into your daily routine, it is essential to take a moment to reflect and review your affirmation practice. This subchapter aims to guide you through this introspective process, allowing you to maximize the benefits of affirmations and enhance your overall well-being.

Reflection is a fundamental aspect of personal growth. By taking the time to reflect on your affirmation practice, you gain insights into the progress you have made, areas that need improvement, and the impact affirmations have had on your life. Begin by finding a quiet and peaceful space where you can be alone with your thoughts. Take a few deep breaths, allowing your mind to settle and become present in the moment. Then, contemplate the following questions:

1. How have affirmations influenced my thoughts and beliefs? Reflect on the changes you have noticed in your thinking patterns and the beliefs you hold about yourself and the world. Consider whether any negative self-talk has diminished, and if positive self-talk has become more prevalent.

2. What positive changes have I witnessed in my life? Think about how affirmations have impacted your daily life. Have you noticed improvements in your relationships, career, health, or overall well-being? Take note of any positive shifts that have occurred as a result of your affirmation practice.

3. Are there any challenges or obstacles I am facing? Acknowledge any areas of your life where you are experiencing difficulties. Consider how affirmations can help you overcome these challenges and develop a plan to incorporate specific affirmations that address these obstacles.

Reviewing your affirmation practice involves examining the techniques and strategies you have been utilizing. Ask yourself the following questions:

1. Am I consistent in practicing affirmations daily? Reflect on your commitment to incorporating affirmations into your routine. Evaluate whether you

have been consistent and identify any obstacles that may be hindering your dedication.

2. Are my affirmations aligned with my goals and values? Review the affirmations you have been using and assess whether they are in alignment with your long-term goals and personal values. Make adjustments as necessary to ensure that your affirmations are guiding you toward your desired outcomes.

3. How can I enhance my affirmation practice? Consider ways in which you can deepen and enrich your affirmation practice. Explore new techniques such as visualization or journaling, or seek inspiration from books, podcasts, or workshops that focus on affirmations.

By reflecting and reviewing your affirmation practice, you gain valuable insights into your progress, identify areas for growth, and refine your approach. Remember, affirmations are an ongoing practice, and consistent dedication will yield the most profound results. Embrace this opportunity for self-reflection and continue to cultivate a positive life through Positive Affirmations.

Chapter 11: Conclusion and Final Thoughts

Embracing a Positive and Affirming Life

In today's fast-paced world, it is easy to get caught up in the chaos and negativity that surrounds us. However, by consciously choosing to embrace a positive and affirming life, we can transform our mindset and create a life filled with joy, abundance, and happiness. This subchapter aims to guide and inspire people from all walks of life to cultivate a positive mindset through the power of daily affirmations.

Affirmations have the incredible ability to rewire our thought patterns and beliefs. They are positive statements that, when repeated consistently, can help us overcome self-doubt, negative thinking, and fear. By incorporating affirmations into our daily routine, we can shift our focus from limitations to possibilities, from despair to hope, and from insecurity to self-assurance.

This subchapter is a treasure trove of empowering affirmations for life. It is designed to cater to diverse niches, providing affirmations tailored to different aspects of life, including self-love, relationships, career, health, and abundance. Each affirmation has been carefully crafted to resonate with the specific needs and aspirations of individuals in these niches.

By reading and reciting these affirmations daily, you will gradually reprogram your subconscious mind, replacing limiting beliefs with empowering ones. Over time, you will notice a profound shift in your thoughts, emotions, and actions. Positive outcomes will begin to manifest in your life, as you attract opportunities, cultivate meaningful relationships, and achieve your goals.

This subchapter provides a collection of affirmations and offers practical guidance on how to incorporate them into your daily routine effectively. It emphasizes the importance of consistency, intention, and belief in Positive Affirmations. Additionally, it explores various techniques such as visualization, meditation, and journaling, which can enhance the effectiveness of affirmations and help you deepen your connection with their transformative power.

Embracing a positive and affirming life is a journey that requires commitment and dedication. This subchapter will serve as your trusted companion, motivating and inspiring you every step of the way. By embracing Positive Affirmations, you will unlock your true potential, live a life filled with gratitude and abundance, and become the best version of yourself.

Remember, every day is an opportunity to affirm your worth, embrace positivity, and create a life that truly reflects your desires and dreams. Start your transformative journey today and experience the incredible power of affirmations in shaping a positive and fulfilling life.

The Power of Consistency and Persistence

In today's fast-paced world, where instant gratification and quick fixes are often sought after, it is easy to overlook the power of consistency and persistence. However, these two qualities are paramount when it comes to achieving success and living a positive life. In this subchapter, we will explore the remarkable power that consistency and persistence hold and how they can transform your life.

Consistency is the key to building lasting habits and reaching your goals. By committing to a consistent routine, you can make small but significant progress every day. Whether it is in your personal or professional life, consistency allows you to stay on track and overcome obstacles that may come your way. It is the fuel that keeps you going, even when the going gets tough.

Persistence, on the other hand, is the unwavering determination to never give up. It is the refusal to be deterred by setbacks or failures. When you are persistent, you understand that success is not an overnight phenomenon, but rather a result of continuous effort and learning from mistakes. Persistence enables you to bounce back from failures, adapt to changes, and keep moving forward towards your goals.

Consistency and persistence go hand in hand. Consistency provides the foundation for persistence, while persistence fuels consistency. Together, they create a powerful synergy that propels you towards your dreams and aspirations.

To harness the power of consistency and persistence, affirmations play a crucial role. Affirmations are positive statements that you repeat to yourself daily, reinforcing your beliefs and goals. By incorporating affirmations into your daily routine, you are programming your mind to stay consistent and persistent.

Repeat affirmations such as "I am committed to consistency in all areas of my life," or "I am persistent in overcoming challenges and achieving my goals." By consistently affirming these positive statements, you are training your mind to stay focused, motivated, and determined.

Remember, consistency and persistence are not about perfection or never making mistakes. They are about showing up every day, putting in the effort, and never giving up. Embrace the power of consistency and persistence, and watch as your life transforms in ways you never thought possible.

Celebrating Your Growth and Progress

In our journey through life, it is essential to take a step back and appreciate the progress we have made. Each day brings new opportunities for growth, and it is crucial to acknowledge and celebrate these accomplishments. This subchapter, titled "Celebrating Your Growth and Progress," aims to remind you of the importance of recognizing your achievements and embracing a positive mindset.

Life is a series of ups and downs, and it is easy to get caught up in the challenges and setbacks. However, by focusing on your growth and progress, you can shift your perspective and cultivate a more positive outlook on life. Celebrating your achievements, no matter how big or small, allows you to build self-confidence and encourages you to continue striving for personal growth.

Affirmations play a significant role in this process. By incorporating positive affirmations into your daily routine, you can reinforce your belief in yourself and your abilities. Affirmations for life can help you stay focused, motivated, and inspired, even during challenging times. They serve as reminders of your potential and encourage you to keep pushing forward.

When celebrating your growth and progress, it is important to acknowledge the efforts you have put into reaching your goals. Take a moment to reflect on the obstacles you have overcome, the skills you have developed, and the lessons you have learned along the way. Recognize the positive changes you have made in your life and the impact they have had on your overall well-being.

Furthermore, celebrating your growth and progress can also inspire and motivate others. By openly recognizing your achievements, you provide a positive example for those around you. Share your success stories and the lessons you have learned, as they have the potential to inspire others on their journeys of personal growth.

Remember, celebrating your growth and progress is not about comparing yourself to others or seeking validation from external sources. It is about acknowledging your unique journey and embracing the person you have become. So, take a moment each day to celebrate your growth, express gratitude for your progress, and continue affirming your positive life.

Spreading Positivity and Inspiring Others

It can be easy to get caught up in negativity and lose sight of the beauty and joy that surrounds us. However, by consciously spreading positivity and inspiring others, we have the power to create a ripple effect of happiness and change. This subchapter explores the incredible impact that affirmations for life can have on our well-being and on those around us.

Affirmations for life are powerful statements that redirect our thoughts and beliefs towards positivity. By repeating these affirmations daily, we can reprogram our minds to focus on the good, embrace optimism, and attract positive experiences into our lives. But the benefits of affirmations go beyond our personal growth; they extend to those we interact with daily.

As we cultivate a positive mindset through affirmations, we naturally radiate positive energy. This energy is contagious and has the potential to uplift and inspire others. When people witness our unwavering positivity and optimism, they are encouraged to adopt a similar mindset themselves. Our words and actions can become a beacon of light in someone's life, reminding them that there is always hope and beauty to be found.

What we do know, by spreading positivity and inspiring others, we contribute to the creation of a supportive and compassionate community. When we genuinely support and uplift others, we create a safe space for growth and healing. By sharing our stories of overcoming challenges and inspiring others to do the same, we create a network of individuals who are united by a common goal: to live a positive and fulfilling life.

Spreading positivity doesn't require grand gestures or profound wisdom. It starts with small acts of kindness, such as offering a genuine compliment or lending a listening ear. It's about being present and showing empathy towards others. Not only that, but it's about celebrating the successes of those around us and being a source of encouragement during their hardships.

General thought is that, spreading positivity and inspiring others through affirmations for life are a transformative practice that benefits not only us but also the people we encounter. By consciously redirecting our thoughts towards positivity, we become catalysts for change and create a ripple effect of happiness and inspiration in our communities. Together, we can build a world that is filled with kindness, compassion, and boundless possibilities.

Appendix: Sample Affirmations for Various Life Areas and Situations

In this subchapter, you will find a collection of powerful affirmations to uplift and empower you in various aspects of your life. These affirmations are designed to help you cultivate a positive mindset and manifest your desires. By using these affirmations consistently, you can create the life you truly desire.

1. Affirmations for Health and Well-being:

- I am healthy and vibrant, and my body is filled with energy.

- Every day, my body becomes stronger and more resilient.

- I nourish my body with wholesome foods, exercise, and self-care.

- I radiate health and vitality in every cell of my being.

- My mind is calm, and my body is at ease.

2. Affirmations for Relationships:

- I attract loving and supportive relationships into my life.

- I am deserving of deep and meaningful connections.

- My relationships are filled with love, understanding, and mutual respect.

- I am a magnet for positive and uplifting people.

- Every day, my relationships grow stronger and more fulfilling.

3. Affirmations for Abundance and Prosperity:

- I am open to receiving abundance in all areas of my life.

- My income is constantly increasing, and I am financially secure.

- I attract opportunities that bring me wealth and prosperity.

- I am grateful for the abundance that flows into my life.

- I live in a universe of infinite possibilities, and I am worthy of all the good that comes my way.

4. Affirmations for Personal Growth and Success:

- I am capable of achieving any goal I set for myself.

- I possess unlimited potential to create the life of my dreams.

- I am confident and fearless in pursuing my passions.

- I embrace challenges as opportunities for growth and learning.

- I am grateful for my experiences, as they have shaped me into who I am today.

5. Affirmations for Inner Peace and Happiness:

- I choose to focus on the present moment and find joy in every situation.

- I release all negative thoughts and emotions, and I embrace peace within.

- I am surrounded by love and happiness, and it radiates from within me.

- I am controlling my happiness, and I decide to be happy every day.

- I am grateful for all the blessings in my life, big and small.

Remember, affirmations are most effective when repeated daily with conviction and belief. Use these sample affirmations as a starting point, and please don't hesitate to personalize them to align with your specific goals and desires. Embrace Positive Affirmations and watch as your life transforms into a positive and fulfilling journey.

Affirmations that help:

In the journey towards living a positive life, affirmations play a powerful role. Affirmations act as a tool to reprogram our minds, replacing negative thoughts with positive ones. By consistently practicing affirmations, we can transform our beliefs, thoughts, and ultimately, our lives. In this subchapter, we will explore various affirmations that can assist people in their quest for a positive life.

1. Self-Love Affirmations:

"I am deserving of love and respect."

"I embrace my uniqueness and love myself unconditionally."

"I am enough, just as I am."

Self-love is the foundation of a positive life. By repeating these affirmations daily, people can cultivate a deep sense of self-acceptance, self-worth, and self-compassion.

2. Gratitude Affirmations:

"I am grateful for all the blessings in my life."

"I appreciate the abundance that surrounds me."

"I choose to focus on the positive aspects of every situation."

Gratitude is a powerful force that can shift our perspective and attract more positivity into our lives. These affirmations help people develop a grateful mindset and appreciate the beauty and abundance present in their everyday experiences.

3. Success Affirmations:

"I am capable of achieving greatness."

"I attract success and abundance effortlessly."

"I have the power to create the life of my dreams."

Success is not only about financial achievements but also about personal growth and fulfillment. These affirmations empower people to believe in their abilities and take inspired actions towards their goals, ultimately leading to a positive and successful life.

4. Health and Well-being Affirmations:

"I am blessed with a healthy mind, body, and spirit."

"I attract vibrant health and vitality into my life."

"I am in perfect alignment with my body's natural healing abilities."

Our well-being encompasses not only physical health but also emotional and mental well-being. By using these affirmations, people can cultivate a positive relationship with their bodies and focus on their overall health, leading to a more fulfilling and positive life.

By incorporating these affirmations into their daily routine, people can gradually shift their mindset, creating a positive ripple effect in all areas of their lives. Affirmations act as a guiding light, reminding individuals of their inherent worth, strength, and potential. Remember, affirmations are most effective when practiced consistently. Therefore, make it a habit to repeat these affirmations with intention, belief, and gratitude each day, and witness the transformative power they hold in creating a positive life.

POSITIVITY

1. I see the good in every situation.
2. My mind is filled with positive thoughts.
3. I believe everything happens for a reason.
4. I transform negative thoughts into positive ones.
5. My life is filled with blessings.

6. I focus on what I can control.
7. Challenges make me stronger.
8. I let go of what I cannot change.
9. Hardships make me more resilient.
10. I find the lesson in each setback.
11. Difficulties lead to personal growth.
12. I can choose to be happy right now.
13. My abilities and talents are unique.
14. I acknowledge my own self-worth.
15. My confidence grows daily.
16. I forgive myself for past mistakes.
17. I have so much to be grateful for.
18. Each day is a fresh start.
19. I surround myself with positive people.
20. Helping others lifts my spirit.
21. I seek out reasons to smile.
22. Laughter makes my soul shine brighter.
23. I see obstacles as opportunities.
24. My mind expands in positivity.
25. I speak words of encouragement.
26. My kindness ripples outwards.
27. I focus on abundance, not lack.
28. My body and mind are perfectly made.
29. I choose progress over perfection.
30. My uniqueness deserves celebrating.
31. Possibilities stretch out before me.
32. I let my light shine brightly.
33. My courage helps me take risks.

34. Challenging assumptions opens my mind.
35. Staying curious keeps me growing.
36. Sharing stories connects me to others.
37. I focus on lifting others up.
38. My patience helps me understand different views.
39. Seeing things anew brings me joy.
40. A smile can change someone's day.
41. I embrace the ever-changing flow of life.
42. Letting go lightens my spirit.
43. I welcome new adventures.
44. The answers I seek are within me.
45. I tune out self-limiting thoughts.
46. My fears do not define me.
47. I welcome inspiration and creativity.
48. Each moment offers me peace.
49. Stepping outside routines renews me.
50. There is beauty in simplicity.
51. My uniqueness deserves celebrating.
52. I focus on abundance, not lack.
53. Possibilities stretch out before me.
54. My courage helps me take risks.
55. Staying curious keeps me growing.
56. Sharing stories connects me to others.
57. Seeing things anew brings me joy.
58. I embrace the ever-changing flow of life.
59. I welcome new adventures.
60. The answers I seek are within me.

61. I tune out self-limiting thoughts.
62. My fears do not define me.
63. Each moment offers me peace.
64. Stepping outside routines renews me.
65. There is beauty in simplicity.
66. I let my light shine brightly.
67. My patience helps me understand different views.
68. A smile can change someone's day.
69. Letting go lightens my spirit.
70. I focus on lifting others up.
71. I believe I have unique talents.
72. My abilities deserve recognition.
73. I celebrate small wins.
74. My self-confidence blossoms each day.
75. I nurture my physical and mental health.
76. My creativity enriches my life.
77. Seeking balance helps me thrive.
78. I welcome inspiration with open arms.
79. My kindness multiplies my joy.
80. I embrace the gifts I've been given.
81. Fresh perspectives widen my vision.
82. New adventures invigorate my spirit.
83. Stepping outside routines awakens me.
84. Simplicity helps me appreciate what matters.
85. Letting go of clutter clears my mind.
86. I focus my energy on what's meaningful.
87. Listening expands my understanding.

88. I welcome growth and self-discovery.
89. My unique voice deserves to be heard.
90. I nurture my body, mind and soul.
91. My authentic self is good enough.
92. I lovingly accept myself as I am.
93. My unique gifts enrich the world.
94. I deserve to take up space.
95. My light makes the world brighter.
96. I embrace my magical weirdness.
97. Quirks make me wonderfully me.
98. I celebrate the things that set me apart.
99 I shine just by being myself.
100. I choose to focus on the positive.

HEALTH

1. I make time to nourish my body.
2. I have the energy I need to thrive.
3. My body is getting healthier every day.
4. I embrace habits that serve me well.
5. My food choices make me feel good.
6. I release tension from my body and mind.
7. Exercise brings me joy and vitality.
8. Movement makes me feel alive.
9. I enjoy being active and outdoors.
10. I move in ways that make my body feel great.
11. My body appreciates how I care for it.

12. I have excellent physical health and stamina.
13. Health and strength infuse every muscle.
14. Vitality flows freely through me.
15. My body grows stronger each day.
16. I gently stretch and strengthen my muscles.
17. My body gracefully becomes more flexible.
18. I fill my lungs fully and breathe easily.
19. Relaxation washes over me like a soft wave.
20. My energy is restored through rest.
21. I make positive choices to nourish my body.
22. Healthy habits come easily to me.
23. I enjoy being physically active every day.
24. My body thrives on balanced self-care.
25. I appreciate all that my body does for me.
26. My body heals quickly from injury or strain.
27. I have optimal physical and mental energy.
28. Vibrant health is my natural state.
29. My constitution grows more resilient each day.
30. Wellbeing radiates through my entire being.
31. My body loves how I care for it.
32. Adequate rest recharges me completely.
33. Hydration renews every cell.
34. Nutrition gives me what I need to thrive.
35. I heal by listening to body's wisdom.
36. Exercise enhances strength, health and joy.
37. I move in ways that serve me beautifully.
38. My body flourishes with self-care.
39. I make time to nourish body and soul.

40. My fitness routine makes me feel empowered.
41. My unique body shape is perfectly fine.
42. I accept my body as it is right now.
43. My body expresses health and radiance.
44. Positive habits support my fitness goals.
45. Living actively energizes my spirit.
46. I appreciate all my body does for me.
47. My body grows stronger step by step.
48. I care for my health with compassion.
49. My dedication inspires my highest health.
50. I celebrate each sign of vitality within.

RELATIONSHIPS

Personal Relationships
1. I nurture relationships that inspire growth.
2. I give and receive care freely in relationships.
3. I communicate openly and honestly with loved ones.
4. I set healthy boundaries in my close connections.
5. I embrace trust and vulnerability.
6. I choose to see the best in my loved ones.
7. My kindness uplifts my personal relationships.
8. I listen closely to understand perspectives.

9. I speak gently even in disagreement.
10. My forgiveness heals relationships.

WORK RELATIONSHIPS

11. I collaborate effectively at work.
12. I seek first to understand others' views.
13. My professional connections expand my growth.
14. I communicate clearly with colleagues.
15. I build trust through reliability.
16. I accept work relationships gracefully as they change.
17. I embrace teamwork and staff continuity.
18. I share recognition generously.
19. I model integrity for coworkers.
20. My patience enables working relationships to thrive.
21. I contribute positively to company culture.
22. I resolve conflict with empathy and care.
23. Professional bonds strengthen our organization.
24. My warmth puts coworkers at ease.
25. I value all roles that allow our team to flourish.
26. I acknowledge brilliant ideas from colleagues.
27. My words foster an atmosphere of inspiration.
28. I offer assistance openly to coworkers.

29. I express sincere gratitude for my team's efforts.
30. I release judgement about other's work styles.
31. Curiosity expands my perspective on challenges.
32. My flexibility allows growth through change.
33. I share knowledge to lift up fellow colleagues.
34. My dedication motivates those working with me.
35. I embrace workplace relationships as opportunities.
36. My demeanor invites trust from coworkers.
37. I accept imperfections in myself and others gracefully.
38. I compliment strengths I observe in colleagues.
39. I contribute warmth to my work environment.
40. My empathy builds workplace cohesion.
41. I start each day intending to add value for others.
42. I hold myself accountable while extending grace to colleagues.
43. I celebrate team accomplishments wholeheartedly.
44. I acknowledge efforts even greater than results achieved.
45. I embrace that each person strengthens our organization uniquely.

46. I release jealousy and comparisons with coworkers.
47. I remember every role is essential to organizational success.
48. I express care for colleagues both professionally and personally.
49. I honor all who allow our team to thrive.
50. My words sow seeds of encouragement and inspiration.

CONFUSED

Here are 50 positive affirmations for when you feel confused:

1. It's okay that I don't have all the answers right now.
2. Confusion means my mind is opening up to new insights.
3. I give myself permission not to know.
4. With patience, clarity will come in time.
5. This is a chance to get curious.
6. I trust my inner wisdom to guide me.
7. Uncertainty helps me stay flexible and adaptive.
8. Charging ahead isn't always the best path forward.
9. Sitting with confusion builds understanding.

10. Being at peace with not knowing opens me to learn.

11. I release the need to control everything.

12. Progress often lives on the other side of confusion.

13. I embrace the mystery and discovery in each moment.

14. My perspective continues expanding.

15. I give confusion space to transform into insight.

16. Confusion inspires me to see things in new ways.

17. In stillness, clarity will come.

18. I seek understanding from within.

19. With patience, answers will be revealed.

20. This is an opportunity to get really creative.

21. Being unsure of my next step is perfectly okay.

22. Confusion means breakthroughs and growth lie ahead.

23. I let go of self-judgement for not already knowing.

24. Each experience expands my capacity to understand.

25. I allow my mind to sit with uncertainty.

26. Being confused simply means I have more to learn.

27. The confusion will pass if I don't cling too tightly to it.
28. I give myself grace on this journey of expansion.
29. I release the need to control everything.
30. Answers take time to percolate sometimes.
31. Growth lives outside my comfort zone.
32. I let intuition be my guide.
33. Confusion inspires me to open my mind.
34. I embrace new ways of thinking.
35. In time, the pieces will fall into place.
36. I stay open to paradox and ambiguity.
37. Progress builds in unexpected ways.
38. I allow fluidity and flexibility of thought.
39 I trust I have all I need within me.
40. Clarity will come when the time is right.
41. Confusion leads to breaking through barriers.
42. I let this motivate me rather than overwhelm me.
43. I release attachment to specific outcomes.
44. Confusion means I'm learning and growing.
45. I let go and let understanding emerge.
46. I give myself permission to reorder my reality.
47. I embrace confusion as part of progress.
48. Uncertainty brings unlimited possibility.
49. I know clarity will replace this confusion.
50. Being unsure means I stay open and curious.

FEAR

1. I let go of fear and trust in my inner wisdom.
2. I am safe and at peace in this moment.
3. Fear will not overwhelm me.
4. My courage is more powerful than any fear.
5. I have the strength to overcome this.
6. Worrying does not serve me. I let the fear go.
7. Everything will be alright in the end.
8. I choose faith over fear.
9. My fears do not define or control me.
10. I can move through this fearful time.
11. Courage and confidence are awakening within me.
12. I can face each situation as it comes.
13. I relax knowing I can handle what arises.
14. I give my worries away to the universe.
15. All is well even when life feels uncertain.

16. I breathe calmly and stay present in the now.
17. My inner power keeps me feeling safe.
18. This fear will soon melt away.
19. Letting go is allowing light to enter.
20. Any anxiety I feel is only temporary.
21. Solutions exist outside my comfort zone.
22. Each breath makes me feel more at ease.
23. I have the love, wisdom and resources within.
24. My soul is stronger than any struggle or worry.

25. I let faith cast out all fear.
26. Progress begins when I move through discomfort.
27. I walk forward with courage despite uncertainty.
28. My safe space lies within whenever fear surrounds me.
29. Even when afraid, I persevere knowing I will be okay.
30. I allow grace and optimism to overcome this fear.
31. Fear cannot break my serenity and peace of mind.
32. I welcome calm and clarity instead of anxiety.
33. My worthiness remains unchanged by any struggle.
34. I have survived each fearful time before this one.
35. Each breath makes me feel more at ease.
36. Fear cannot control or diminish my light.
37. I move patiently knowing answers will come.
38. My vision is greater when I let go of apprehension.
39. I am stronger than anything that brings me dread.
40. Clarity and courage are already within me.
41. I let faith conquer each worry and concern.

42. Solutions shine brightly once fear moves aside.

43. Any anxiety I feel is only temporary.

44. My inner resilience helps me feel safe again.

45. I embrace self-care to soothe my worried mind.

46. Staying hopeful lifts my outlook higher.

47. I give my burdens away to the universe.

48. Each step forward makes the next one easier.

49. My soul knows I have the strength inside.

50. I allow love to cast out all fear.

DOUBT

1. I let go of self-doubt and embrace my inner wisdom.

2. I believe in my abilities even when doubt arises.

3. Fear and doubt cannot break my confidence.

4. Challenges help me grow stronger and wiser.

5. My self-worth remains unchanged by setbacks.

6. I welcome clarity, seeing past any confusion.

7. Solutions shine brightly once doubt moves aside.

8. Progress begins when I move through discomfort.

9. My vision is greater when I let doubts fade.

10. I focus on strengths not lack of confidence.

11. With patience, I know I will find my way.

12. I trust in my talents and unique gifts.

13. My courage is more powerful than any fear.
14. I forgive myself when I make mistakes.
15. Overcoming obstacles builds resilience.
16. My confidence grows with each lesson learned.
17. Self-trust anchors me when doubts arise.
18. I let my light shine brightly.
19. Staying hopeful lifts my outlook higher.
20. I welcome inspiration and clarity.
21. Each step forward makes the next easier.
22. What I seek lies just outside comfort zones.
23. My fear does not define or limit me.
24. Progress manifests wonders when I persist.
25. Solutions shine brightly once doubts fade.
26. I choose to focus on strengths not weaknesses.
27. My sense of self-worth deepens daily.
28. Conquering doubts strengthens my confidence.
29. With compassion, I quiet my inner critic.
30. Each experience expands my capacity.
31. My unique talents add value to the world.
32. I let successes strengthen and failures instruct.
33. Courage and confidence are awakening within.
34. My big dreams deserve pursuing despite doubts.
35. Obstacles can magnify purpose and resilience.
36. I give my worries away to the universe.

37. Through uncertainty, I keep moving forward.
38. My vision expands when I release expectations.
39. Progress often begins with "I don't know".
40. Solutions shine brightly once doubts fade.
41. My self-belief grows stronger each time I persist.
42. I welcome inspiration and breakthroughs.
43. My self-confidence is not easily shaken.
44. Each small win fans my inner spark into flame.
45. I let go of doubt and embrace possibility.
46. My abilities deserve recognition.
47. Temporary failure helps me grow.
48. With compassion, I quiet my inner critic.
49. Courage awakens when I leave comfort zones.
50. I believe in my talents and capacity.

MOTIVATION

1. I trust myself to make the right decision; I have the tools and abilities that I need to do so.
2. I am becoming closer to my true self every day; every challenge, loss, and success brings me closer to that goal.
3. I am learning valuable lessons from myself every day, and I will continue to keep trying to learn from myself.

4. I am the architect of my life; I build its foundation and choose its contents.
5. Today, I am brimming with energy and overflowing with joy; these are emotions I can use to motivate myself throughout the day.
6. My body is healthy; my mind is brilliant; my soul is tranquil; this shall provide me with the alignment I need to conquer the tasks ahead of me today.
7. I am superior to negative thoughts and low actions.
8. I have been given endless talents, which I begin to utilize today, and I have the confidence to do so.
9. I forgive those who have harmed me in my past and peacefully detach from them.
10. I allow myself to be who I am without judgment because that is what is going to allow me to be happiest in my life.
11. I listen to my intuition and trust my inner guide because that is going to take me closer to what makes me truly happy.
12. My drive and ambition allow me to achieve my goals because I have a fire inside of me pushing me forward.
13. I possess the qualities needed to be extremely successful, and I have the confidence to apply those skills in ways that will enable my success.
14. Creative energy surges through me and leads me to new and brilliant ideas.

15. My ability to conquer my challenges is limitless; my potential to succeed is infinite.

16. I am courageous, and I stand up for myself and for others who may need my help in doing so because it is the right thing to do.

17. I wake up today with strength in my heart and clarity in my mind that gives me the ability to make good decisions throughout my day.

18. I am at peace with all that has happened, is happening, and will happen.

19. I permit myself to do what is right for me because that is how I allow myself to be the most authentic.

20. I give myself space to grow and learn because I understand that there is always room for growth in our lives.

21. I am blessed with an incredible family and wonderful friends.

22. I acknowledge my self-worth and am willing to improve it in areas that I consider are weaknesses right now.

23. Though these times are difficult, they are only a short phase of life; everything that is happening now is happening for my ultimate good.

24. My efforts are being supported by those around me who also want to see me succeed and do amazing things.

25. My obstacles are moving out of my way; my path is carved towards greatness; I just need to continue walking that path.

26. I am creatively inspired by the world around me, and I can use that inspiration to achieve amazing things in my life.

27. My mind is full of brilliant ideas that I can use to benefit myself and others.

28. I put my energy into things that matter to me because that is what brings me the most happiness in my life.

29. I am at peace with who I am as a person because I understand what is important to me and what is not and live by my values.

30. I make a difference in the world by simply existing in it and trying to make it a better place in whatever ways I can.

31. I am in the process of positive change.

32. I am deeply fulfilled by all that I do.

33. I know that I am already successful.

34. My day begins and ends with gratitude.

35. I am healthy, whole, and complete.

36. I release all negative thoughts of the past and all worries about the future.

37. My life gets better all the time.

38. I am constantly discovering new ways to improve my health.

39. I trust the Universe to help me see the good in everything and in everyone.

40. Money comes to me easily and effortlessly.

41. I trust the process of life.

42. I don't sweat the small stuff.

43. I am in charge of how I feel and today I choose happiness.

44. I am enough.

45. I have the power to create change.

46. I let go of all that no longer serves me.

47. I am brimming with energy and overflowing with joy.

48. My body is healthy; my mind is brilliant; my soul is tranquil.

49. I am full of creative energy and new ideas.

50. I can overcome any challenge I face.

51. I feel joy and contentment in this moment.

52. I feel happy and enthusiastic about life.

53. Every day in every way, I am becoming more and more successful.

54. I know exactly what I need to do to achieve success.

55. I fully accept myself and know that I am worthy of great things in life.

56. I am whole.

57. I fill my mind with positive and nourishing thoughts.

58. I am grounded in the experience of the present moment.
59. I am focused and engaged in the task at hand.
60. I accept and embrace all experiences, even unpleasant ones.
61. I observe my emotions without becoming attached to them.
62. Every day I am more and more at ease.
63. I am calm, happy, and content.
64. If I can change my thoughts, I can change anything.
65. Today I will make progress towards my goals.

HEALING

1. I am filled with vitality and health.
2. I lovingly care for my body's needs.
3. I release the past with compassion.
4. I welcome positive changes.
5. I am transforming in healthy ways.
6. I accept myself as I am.
7. I appreciate my body's resilience.
8. I have faith in my strength.
9. I am gentle with myself during this process.
10. I let go and allow healing to unfold.

11. I act with wisdom and patience.
12. I acknowledge my feelings with care.

13. I nourish my spirit through nature and arts.
14. Creativity brings me joy and renewal.
15. I give myself permission to rest.
16. Peacefulness resides within me.
17. I am worthy of wellness and wholeness.
18. My afflictions are temporary teachers.
19. I infuse my thoughts with optimism.
20. Each day brings me closer to health.
21. I release fears about the future.
22. I live fully in each moment.
23. My body regenerates itself every day.
24. I welcome miracles large and small.
25. The answers I seek reside within.
26. I allow healing visions to inspire me.
27. I forgive all pains of my past.
28. I have courage to transform difficulties into growth.
29. Nature's beauty fills me with awe.
30. Music and arts feed my soul.
31. My dreams guide me to inner truths.
32. I compassionately nurture all aspects of my being.
33. My community supports my wellbeing.
34. I allow loving kindness to soften my heart.
35. I choose to see life's beauty, even in darkness.
36. I release judgment and open my eyes to wonder.

37. I consciously generate thoughts which enable my healing.
38. I lovingly accept support others offer me.
39. I welcome rest as an essential part of my healing process.
40. I trust that I have all I need within and around me for complete healing.

LOVE

1. I let go of barriers to love.
2. I love myself and others equally.
3. I deserve abundant love.
4. Loving relationships fill my life.
5. I give and receive unconditional love.
6. More loving relationships come to me.
7. My soulmate seeks me as I seek them.
8. I welcome more romance.
9. My new partner enjoys laughter and fun with me.
10. We know the joy of mutual love and respect.
11. I welcome passion and romance.
12. Emotional intimacy comes naturally in my relationship.
13. Conflicts are resolved respectfully.
14. I have healthy boundaries and feel secure.
15. My relationship grows stronger every day.
16. My partner is my soulmate.

17. I believe in myself and my abilities.

18. I love my unique qualities.

19. I blossom more beautifully each day.

20. My dreams manifest.

21. I learn from challenges.

22. I feel confident in any situation.

23. I imagine and see the best in myself.

24. I accomplish anything I focus on.

25. I am incredibly intelligent.

26. I inspire others with my inner love.

27. I deserve love, success and happiness.

28. My heart radiates love openly.

29. I give my heart and receive another's in return.

30. I am loved more than I imagined.

31. I make room for an amazing partner.

32. The Universe brings my soulmate.

33. My partner shows deep, passionate love.

34. I am in a wonderful relationship.

35. I deserve affection.

36. I attract the perfect person for me.

37. My partner loves me as I am.

38. I deserve a happy relationship.

39. I am overwhelmed with love!

40. I am open to receive love.

FEELING DOWN AND DEPRESSED

1. I am valued even when I'm not productive.

2. I am loved despite my temporary sadness.

3. I do the best I can.

4. I am appreciated.

5. I am needed.

6. I am not my depression.

7. I'm not the label of depression.

8. I have persevered and persevered and should celebrate my tenacity.

9. I am strong.

10. I am much more than I give myself credit for.

11. My brain is my friend.

12. My discomfort won't last forever.

13. I am resilient.

14. I am a silent warrior.

15. I am okay where I am right now.

16. I love myself unconditionally.

17. I am STRONG!

18. I allow only healthy and loving relationships into my life.

19. Life wants the best for me.

20. I am OK with where I am right now.

21. I am connected and comfortable in all environments, with all people.

22. I find and enjoy the simple pleasures life is offering right now.

23. How I feel matters, therefore I concentrate on aspects of life that make me feel good!

24. My challenges bring me better opportunities.
25. My mood creates a physiological response in my body. I am peaceful and positive!
26. I am in control of my thoughts and my life.
27. I love myself and who I am.
28. I am strong.
29. I am worthy.
30. I am courageous.
31. I am beautiful inside and out.
32. I am brave.
33. I am a survivor.
34. I am focused.
35. I am determined.
36. I am full of life.
37. I am a positive person.
38. I trust myself.
39. I love myself.
40. I am happy.
41. I am vibrant.
42. I am loving.
43. I am generous.
44. I am humble.
45. I am grateful.

SUCCESS

1. I am grateful for everything that is good in my world.

2. I deserve the very best in every aspect of my life.
3. Every day I experience the joy of receiving and giving abundance.
4. When I go after what I want, it comes to me.
5. I always dress for success in mind, body, and spirit.
6. Wonderful things are happening to me.
7. Everything I touch is a success.
8. I celebrate my success.
9. I have successful relationships.
10. I am creating an amazing life.
11. I see the challenges in my life as opportunities to grow.
12. I am highly motivated and productive.
13. It doesn't matter what others think of me, for I know who I am.
14. Success comes easily to me.
15. I am transforming into a more successful person.
16. I create the life I want.
17. Today, I am brimming with energy and overflowing with joy.
18. I am becoming better every single day.
19. I am worthy of manifesting my biggest desires.
20. It is impossible for me to fail.
21. I am in charge of my destiny.
22. I am creating the life of my dreams.
23. If I put my mind to it, I achieve it.

24. I have the power to create all the success and prosperity I desire.

25. I let go of old, negative beliefs that have stood in the way of my success.

26. My mind is free of resistance and open to exciting new possibilities.

27. I am motivated to go after my dreams.

28. I make good decisions.

29. My mind is a magnet for all good things.

30. I am worthy of all the good life has to offer, and I deserve to be successful.

31. I believe in myself and my ability to succeed.

32. I am grateful for all my skills and talents that serve me so well.

33. Life just keeps getting better and better.

34. I am enjoying my work today and optimistic about the coming days.

35. The universe is filled with endless opportunities for me and my career.

36. I am surrounded by positive, supportive people who believe in me.

37. I am always open minded and eager to explore new avenues to success.

38. I am a magnet for success.

39. I recognize opportunity when it knocks and seize the moment.

40. Every day I discover interesting and exciting new paths to pursue.

41. I am surrounded by abundance.
42. When I need help, I effortlessly attract the perfect resources and solutions.
43. Everywhere I look, I see prosperity.
44. I am well organized and manage my time with expert efficiency.
45. I was born to be successful; it's my natural state of being.
46. I am committed to achieving success in every area of my life.
47. I love my job, and my work is a fulfilling part of my journey to greater success.
48. My ambitions are in perfect alignment with my personal values.
49. I work with fascinating, inspiring people who all share my enthusiasm.
50. By creating success for myself I am creating success and opportunities for others.

ENERGY

1. Every cell in my body vibrates with positive energy.
2. Every cell in my body is happy, healthy, relaxed, and at peace.
3. I have an aura of positive energy surrounding me at all times.

4. I am relaxed and open to attracting positive energy from the Universe.

5. The Universe guides me in miraculous ways.

6. My life is filled with perfect synchronicities.

7. I am happy, I am healthy, I am content, I am peaceful, I am prosperous, I am abundant, I am infinite consciousness.

8. I am connected to the whole. I am one with the Sun, the Earth, the Air, the Universe. I am Life Itself.

9. I effortlessly let go of thoughts that drain me and refocus my attention on thoughts that empower me.

10. I know that my body is a manifestation of pure spirit, and that spirit is perfect, and therefore my body is perfect.

11. The Universe is sending me so many opportunities. I enjoy prioritizing those that will create the highest vision I have for my life.

12. My inner world is filled with positivity and it reflects in my outer world. I bring calm, joy and positivity everywhere I am.

13. I see the hand of divine intelligence all around me, in the flower, the tree, the brook, the meadow.

14. What most fulfills & energizes me is what manifests in my life. I let go of everything not divinely designed for me, and the perfect plan of my life now comes to pass.

15. Each day, I let go of limiting beliefs and focus on empowering beliefs that help me reach my greatest potential.

16. I am an alchemist; I have the power to transform negative energy into positive energy.

17. I am constantly growing and upgrading myself. I am becoming more conscious, understanding and self-aware each day.

18. I am a magnet for positive energy.

19. I give out positive energy and attract positive energy in return.

20. I am healthy, wealthy, powerful, strong, confident, fearless, successful and blessed.

21. I am calm, relaxed, balanced, free, open and peaceful. I am one with the Universe.

22. I am love, I am joy, I am happiness, I am rich, I am prosperous, I am wise, I am abundance.

23. Today is a new day and a new opportunity to start fresh on a good note.

24. Today represents a day for a new beginning and I greet the day with fresh eyes and a fresh mind.

25. Abundance flows through my day—I have all the happiness, love and positive energy I need today to have the most amazing day.

26. In this moment, I give myself permission to release bad and toxic thoughts and allow the good energy to flow in.

27. I feel so much joy and happiness in this moment and radiate that energy throughout my day.

28. I feel beautiful inside and out today and define my own beauty through my positive energy, happiness and abundance of love.

29. This abundance of love and positive energy allows me to step into my day able to accomplish all that I can, into my mission, into my words and into this moment.

30. Today I allow myself to feel the good that surrounds me, stay positive throughout the day as the positive energy is flowing throughout my body and nourish my body with the nutrients it needs.

31. I will not allow negative thinking to penetrate my thoughts, dictate my decision making, or intimidate my hope for the future.

32. I surround myself with people who lift me up, speak life into my vision and purpose, and who bring out the best in me.

33. I am a bearer of light casting out the darkness.

34. Negativity has no choice but to leave when I am present.

35. I focus my energy on things that add value to my life.

36. I am committed to resting my energy when I feel myself getting lost in negative thought.

37. I am intentional about the energy I put out and the energy I allow around me.

38. Today, I am brimming with energy and over-flowing with joy. These are emotions I can use to motivate myself throughout the day.

39. I am superior to negative thoughts and low actions.

40. I listen to my intuition and trust my inner guide because that is going to take me closer to what makes me truly happy.

41. My drive and ambition allow me to achieve my goals because I have a fire inside of me pushing me forward.

42. Creative energy surges through me and leads me to new and brilliant ideas.

43. I put my energy into things that matter to me because that is what brings me the most happiness in my life.

44. I am vibrant. I use my time and energy wisely.

45. I share my talents with the world by feeling energized.

46. I am good at helping others feel energized.

47. I put my energy into things that matter to me.

48. I am grateful to have people in my life who boost my energy and vitality.

49. The Universe will guide me on anything and everything divinely.

50. My mind and body are in complete alignment with the Universe.

SELF ESTEEM

1. Abundance fills my life with wonderful people and experiences.
2. I enjoy prosperous living in body, mind, and spirit.
3. Thank you. Thank you. THANK YOU! I have such an amazing life.
4. Happiness is my birthright, I am worthy of all the good life has to offer and accept it now.
5. I have everything I need to be happy right now.
6. I am focused on enjoying life, and I find happiness wherever I look.
7. I am effortlessly attracting health, wealth, happiness, and love.
8. Abundance flows through my day—I have all the happiness, love and positive energy I need today to have the most amazing day.
9. I feel so much joy and happiness at this moment and radiate that energy throughout my day.
10. Every day in every way I am feeling happier and happier.
11. I give myself permission to let go and be happy right now.
12. I am so grateful now that I am a magnet for miracles, happiness, and joy.
13. Today, I am allowing the energy of happiness to flow through me and fill me with joy.

14. I choose to be happy and grateful today.
15. I am surrounded by people who love and support me.
16. I can brighten up anyone's bad day.
17. I can make a difference in this world.
18. I will face my fear and get out of my comfort
zone.
19. I have a brave heart and a brave soul.
20. It is okay to make mistakes and not know
everything.
21. I am excited to learn new things today.
22. I am aware of my gift to the world and share it
freely.
23. I am compassionate with others and myself.
24. I am a positive being, aware of my potential.
25. There are no blocks I cannot overcome.
26. I love to meet other people and make new
friends.
27. I am my best source of motivation.
28. Challenges are opportunities to grow and improve.
29. I attract positive people into my life.
30. I make a difference by showing up every day
and doing my best.
31. I am becoming a better version of myself one
day at a time.
32. I am worthy of having what I want.
33. I am grateful for my journey and its lessons.

34. I accept compliments easily.

35. Everything is possible.

36. I am creative and open to new solutions.

37. I choose to embrace the mystery of life.

38. I already have what I need.

39. What I want is already here or on its way.

40. I appreciate all that I have.

41. I allow everything to be as it is.

42. I enjoy going with the flow.

43. The more I let go, the better I feel.

44. I live from a place of abundance.

45. I release anything that doesn't serve me.

46. I believe in my abilities and express my true self with ease.

47. All I need is within me.

48. I am stronger than I seem.

49. I am braver than I think.

50. I have unshakable faith.

51. Miracles are taking place in my life.

52. I love and accept myself for who I am.

53. I radiate and receive love and respect.

54. I am loved and respected wherever I go.

55. I am unique in my talents and abilities and do not need validation from others.

56. People see value in my services and I am rewarded graciously.

57. I am self-reliant, creative and persistent in whatever I do.

58. I deserve all that is good.

59. I am grateful for all the wonderful things in my life.

60. I am full of loving, healthy, positive and prosperous thoughts which eventually convert into my life experiences.

61. I am unique and my dreams and aspirations are unique to myself. I do not need to prove myself to anyone.

62. I am solution driven. Every problem is a chance to grow.

63. I am never alone in my pursuit of success. The universe supports me in expected and unexpected ways.

64. I am not a prisoner of the past and live only in the moment. That way I enjoy life to the fullest.

65. I am not a Tree and have the power to change myself how I see fit.

66. Only I am responsible for making my choices and decisions.

67. I am not selfish in giving priority to my desires.

68. Every moment brings us a choice and I choose happiness no matter what my circumstances.

69. I am flexible and open to new experiences.

70. I think positively and expect the best.

The affirmations cover a wide range of areas, including self-worth, gratitude, confidence, resilience, success, and abundance to name a few. They remind readers of their inherent worthiness and the power they possess to attract positive experiences and opportunities. Furthermore, they encourage individuals to release negativity, overcome challenges, and trust in themselves and the universe.

The book recognizes that positivity is not just a fleeting state of mind but a way of life. It emphasizes the importance of focusing on the present moment, embracing change, and being open to receiving love and support. Through these affirmations, readers are encouraged to celebrate their accomplishments, appreciate the beauty of life, and become sources of inspiration to others.

Whether read daily, used as mantras during meditation, or displayed as reminders in visible places, these affirmations serve as powerful tools for cultivating a positive mindset. They offer guidance and encouragement, helping individuals navigate through life's ups and downs with optimism and resilience. By incorporating these affirmations into their daily routines, readers can create a positive foundation for long-lasting personal growth and a more fulfilling life.

Thank You for reading. I have many other self help and self Improvement books, from psychology to fitness. All available at book retailers. You can find my book portfolio at:

kevinbdibacco.crevado.com

www.ingramcontent.com/pod-product-compliance
Lightning Source LLC
Chambersburg PA
CBHW070521160726
48003CB00004B/1656